Preface

Giorgio Agamben is one of the most hotly debated political philosophers of today. Among other things, he is famous for restating Walter Benjamin's thesis that the state of exception is becoming permanent. This thesis goes on to say that the democracies of today, with their focuses on the rule of law and on human rights, in reality are constructed upon a constitutive and permanent state of exception, in which no rights are guaranteed. Hence, Agamben's project is a total restructuring of modern political thought: instead of building upon the idea of a citizen, it should be built with the idea of the stateless human being, who has been stripped of all rights, as its point of departure.

But Agamben is not only a political philosopher. His works deal with all the classic philosophical problems. What is being? What is a human being? What is life? What is law? What is justice? His way of treating these problems, however, is quite different from the ordinary academic way of doing things. Agamben tends to write a different kind of text than the very schematized articles for academic journals that tend to be the norm. Instead, his texts are often essayistic and broken up into small fragmented reflections filled with digressions and references to all of his immense literary, historical, philosophical, theological and juridical knowledge. In more recent years and especially with the *Homo Sacer* series, he has produced more concise academic treatises that develop their theme and argument over a greater number of pages. Still, Agamben's style is both dense and convoluted. His works are never easy to engage with.

This is the reason for my writing this book. I aim to show that Agamben's works are both pertinent and, once one gets acquainted with his particular style, far from as obscure as they have from time to time been accused of being. I will argue that it is precisely in the radicality of Agamben's thought that we find some crucial and very useful ideas that challenge the most fundamental and unquestioned assumptions, the most fundamental doxas, that frame the practice of thought as we know it in the science, law, politics and economics of the West. Thus, when Agamben is accused of obscurity (see e.g. Scheuerman 2006, p.69), I would argue that it is in fact because the accuser is helplessly caught within the frame of thought that Agamben is diagnosing and criticizing in his works, at least in part.

Some themes that are important for Agamben's philosophy have been left out of this book; thus, for instance, the concept of nudity is not discussed here. Other crucial themes are underplayed or receive less attention than they rightly deserve. The theme of language might, for instance, deserve to play a greater role than I am capable of giving it here. The first reason for these and other omissions is the intended scope of the book; it is meant to be short and accessible and thus it cannot deal with everything. A second reason is that I have chosen what I believe is the most crucial theme of Agamben's thinking as the one around which I structure my presentation: this theme is ontology. I think that the best way of understanding Agamben's philosophy as a comprehensive whole, while at the same time avoiding the pitfalls that certain commentators and critics tend to fall into, is to have the ontological background of his thought in the back of one's mind whenever one reads his texts. By taking this path I hope to present, as clearly as possible, the crucial ideas, arguments and lines of thought of Agamben's political philosophy.

Acknowledgments

I would like to thank Carlsbergfondet for its generous support of my research (see www.carlsbergfondet.dk). Without it this book would not have become a reality.

Introduction: Ontology as Political Theory

> On 31 December 2003 Khaled el Masri boarded a bus in Ulm, Germany, with a view to visiting Skopje in order, as is stated, 'to take a short vacation and some time off from a stressful home environment'. At around 3 PM he arrived at the Serbian Macedonian border crossing at Tabanovce (ECHR Grand Chamber 2012).

In this most factual and quiet way begins the story of el Masri's ordeal, as noted by the European Court of Human Rights. At Tabanovce, el Masri was detained by Macedonian police officers. He did not regain his freedom until several months later. On May 24, 2004, he was set free in Albania near the Serbian and Macedonian borders. Until then, he had been held incommunicado, questioned, handed over to a CIA rendition team, tortured, transported to a prison in Afghanistan known as 'The Salt Pit', and further tortured until he was flown back to Europe and set free in Albania in what seems to have been a misguided attempt at a cover-up.

We know these things to be facts because of the work of the European Court of Human Rights and because of the work of the Committee on Legal Affairs and Human Rights under the Council of Europe. Rapporteur Dick Marty of Switzerland has had a crucial role in uncovering the facts of the case. He has furthermore proven the complicity of several European states in similar cases, and he has provided substantial evidence to the fact that the US has organized and operated a covert 'rendition network' which spans the entire globe for the sole purpose of detaining, transporting, questioning and torturing potential so-called 'persons of interest' in the global war on terror.

As problematic—and indeed scandalous—as such a network may seem, and as tragic as the individual cases such as that of el Masri, may be, these facts serve primarily to force us to think about all the things we do not know about. El Masri had his life torn apart, but at least he had his day in court. The mere existence of the rendition network, which Marty calls 'a spider's nest', indicates that many others have suffered similar or worse fates that we know nothing about.

In this way, the case shows us both the strengths and the weakness of juridical thought. El Masri's life is in ruins. He has certainly had his day in court, and the ruling was in his favour in the end. But that does not mean that his life is not in ruins. His case has taken many years to process, and it was never recognized by the US legal system, where it has been dismissed at every step of the legal system. The Eastern District of Virginia dismissed the case, 'finding that the US Government had validly asserted the State secrets privilege', the United States Court of Appeals confirmed that decision and the Supreme Court refused to review the case (ECHR Grand Chamber 2012 I,D,2). Furthermore, the case of el Masri is the first, and to date, the only case that has gone this far. The European Court of Human Rights is the oldest and most renowned international court of human rights, but it is the first time that a case of this magnitude has reached a verdict. Yet we know from el Masri's story and from the investigations of Dick Marty that many others share his fate.

The point is that the very fact that the ECHR has ruled in his favour and cleared his name gives us a feeling that justice has been served. And in a way it has. The European Court of Human Rights was unanimous, clear and extremely harsh in its condemnations of the actions of Macedonia and its US accomplices. But it seems hard to escape the feeling that this is a strange form of justice. Furthermore, it seems very unlikely that any kind of legal action will ever be taken against the true culprits in cases such as this one. And what is even worse, the case only serves as indication that so many others are left to linger in the black holes and grey areas that seem to emerge everywhere whenever the issues of security and legality clash. If justice can be said to have been served in the el Masri case, then this cannot but leave us with the notion that our form of justice is unjust.

Giorgio Agamben: Political Philosophy

Giorgio Agamben: Political Philosophy

Rasmus Ugilt

$\mathcal{HEB}$ ☼ **Humanities-Ebooks**

First published by *Humanities-Ebooks, LLP,*
Tirril Hall, Tirril, Penrith CA10 2JE

The Pdf Ebook is available to private purchasers from http://www.humanities-ebooks.co.uk and to libraries from Ebrary, EBSCO and MyiLibrary.com.

ISBN 978-1-84760-337-1 Pdf Ebook
ISBN 978-1-84760-338-8 Paperback
ISBN 978-1-84760-339-5 Kindle Ebook
ISBN 978-1-84760-340-1 ePub Ebook

Contents

Agamben's Philosophical Method

The political philosophy of Giorgio Agamben sets out from the recognition of this problem. Whatever organized systems of legality, politics and morality we put our faith in today, when we are confronted with the ultimate problems of our social and political lives, it seems as if we always tend to miss something crucial. No matter what we do, it seems as if justice is never quite served. Why is that?

In the end, for Agamben, the answer to this question is not to be found within legal scholarship, nor is it to be found within political or social science. That much is clear from his scornful motto in *State of Exception*: '*quare siletis juristiæ in munere vestro*' (Why are you jurist silent about that which matters the most to you?). If the question is left unanswered by legal scholarship this may be because answering it, in Agamben's view, requires a way of thinking that has traditionally been at home in philosophy. Two philosophical endeavours are crucial for understanding how Agamben treats the question. The first is ontology and the second is genealogy.

Ontology

Ontology is the most fundamental philosophical discipline. It concerns the question of being qua being, which is the definition given by Aristotle in a famous passage of the *Metaphysics* (Aristotle 1960, p.1003a). For Aristotle this meant that ontology deals with the most fundamental way of asking the question: what is being? To him, all other sciences dealt in questions of being that are less fundamental and less general. Biology, for instance, deals with the question of being, in the way that it asks: what is being insofar as it is living being? And physics deals with the question of being in the way that it asks: what is a being insofar as it is a physical being?

Today, an unfortunate commonsensical scientism has it that the most fundamental question of being is identical to the most fundamental question of physics. This is a mistake. The problem here is not physics, but rather the philosophical interpretation of the fundamental question of being entailed in the positing of that identity.

Logically, the question of what being is, qua being and nothing else, must be prior to the question of what being is insofar as it is physical being. The mere fact that physics deals with the entities that are the smallest, the largest or which contain the highest amount of energy, does not mean that physical entities are the most fundamental. That is the case, simply because it is not at all given that everything which is (i.e. has being) must be understood as an entity (or as a thing, or, as the traditional understanding of Aristotle would see it, as a substance). This is a point which in the 20th century has been put most forcefully by the German philosopher Martin Heidegger, from whom Agamben has learned a lot. Using two examples that are crucially important for Agamben, the point can be illustrated by considering the fact that we, in our political and social lives, deal with 'things' such as laws and power, which necessarily must *be*, but which would be understood very poorly if we were to understand them as things or as entities. Put very briefly, the Agambendian approach would instead dictate that we understood them as potentialities (a concept I will explain in greater detail in Chapter 1 below).

Like Heidegger, Agamben treats the fundamental ontological question by returning to Aristotle. In Aristotle he finds some elaborate reflections on ontology that he believes to go against the grain of much of what has been said on the subject of ontology in the millennia that followed the thinking of the ancient Greeks, especially with regard to the concept of potentiality. Agamben separates himself from the thought of Heidegger, however, by following a move that has been more common in French philosophy in the latter part of the 20th century. That is the move that links together the fundamental ontological question about being and what on the surface would seem to be a much more mundane question, that of politics.

In *Homo Sacer: Bare Life and Sovereign Power* (Agamben 1998), Agamben argues that fellow Italian philosopher Antonio Negri has provided the best argument for the linking of politics and ontology with his historical investigation of constituent power in the book that has been translated into English as *Insurgencies* (Negri 1999). Agamben writes of it:

> The strength of Negri's book lies [...] in the final perspective it opens insofar as it shows how constituting power, when conceived in all its radicality, ceases to be a strictly political concept and necessarily presents itself as a category of ontology. The problem of constituting power then becomes the problem of the 'constitution of potentiality' (Agamben 1998, p.44).

Here, we are introduced to the crucial concept in Agamben's political ontology: potentiality. I will, as mentioned, discuss it in greater detail below. In the present chapter, our interest should instead be with the methodological move involved in arguing that a political concept, such as power, is to be investigated in terms of an ontological concept, such as potentiality. To begin with, it will be helpful to make some general and introductory remarks on ontology.

Ontology is certainly not a form of inquiry that is *completely* foreign to other scientific investigations. In fact, every scientific investigation has an ontology in some sense. Indeed, every human practice necessarily entails some ontological frame, which can simply be identified as the most general formulation of what must be said to be in order for that (scientific) practice to be possible. The practice of going to the race-track to bet on horses, for instance, entails an ontology where there are such things as horses, a racetrack, money, rules for betting, etc. More poignantly, the scientific investigation of certain social relations necessitates some crucial assumptions with regard to what constitutes society, e.g. individuals, juridical persons, groups, classes, structures, processes, etc.

A point about these ontological considerations that many would take for granted simply as common sense can be formulated as follows: the determination of the ontological of a certain science or practice must be something very different from the conduct of that practice itself. To make a bet on a horse is something quite different from arguing about what must necessarily be in place in order for such bets to be possible in the first place. Likewise, it is quite a different thing to argue about what society fundamentally consists of than to investigate those things (such as individuals, classes, structures, etc.).

The ultimate point of the direct link between politics and ontology conducted by Agamben and likeminded thinkers is the rejection of this commonsensical distinction. It turns out that one cannot in fact separate the ontology of a practice from the conduct of the practice. Ontology is not just a frame in which a practice is conducted. The strict distinction between an ontological transcendental field and the immanent processes that take place within the field does not hold up. Rather, the ontology of a practice can from time to time emerge directly in the practice that it is the ontological background of. This means that ontology is not simply the passive structure that functions as the medium for events. Rather, it can directly influence and disturb these events as they take place. This may seem like a strange notion, but it should be noted that the point of this manoeuvre is to maintain a strict theoretical monism. It is the rejection of any dualism between the ontological frame and what goes on within it.

As I mentioned above, this link is not simply a fancy idea of a few Italian philosophers (such as Negri and Agamben). It has been a mainstay of a powerful movement in French philosophy in the second half of the 20th century; indeed Negri and Agamben should be viewed as part of this movement. A good way of understanding what is entailed in the philosophical investigation of political ontology can be had from the French philosopher Alain Badiou. In a short article 'The Adventure of French Philosophy' (Badiou 2005). Badiou lists several points that are characteristic of the French movement. The two that are of interest for us are the following:

> A. To abandon the opposition between philosophy of knowledge and philosophy of action, the Kantian division between theoretical and practical reason, and to demonstrate that knowledge itself, even scientific knowledge, is actually a practice;

> B. To situate philosophy directly within the political arena, without making the detour via political philosophy; to invent what I would call the 'philosophical militant', to make philosophy into a militant practice in its presence, in its way of being: not simply a reflection upon politics, but a real political intervention (Badiou 2005, p.76).

The idea of a 'philosophical militant' is in fact simply the direct consequence of the notion that ontology is not to be separated off as a field of inquiry distinct from the reality it describes. Because, if ontology has a direct link to the reality it describes and does not merely serve as a passive transcendental field in which practices take place, then any investigation into political ontology is already a form of political practice. Ultimately, ontology itself is a practice. To think ontologically means to act. Or, as the same point is stated in the first of the theses listed above, there can be no distinction between theoretical and practical reason.

As Badiou points out, this very fact has a profound influence on the very idea of political philosophy. Here, the point that we do not need a practical philosophy to mediate between ontology and political thought becomes crucial. What this means is that a certain more or less implicit hierarchy within the philosophical disciplines has to be abolished. Instead of a hierarchy of thought that puts the most fundamental thinking of being as such at the top, submitting the thinking of a human being to that and the actual practice of organizing what is good and bad for such a being (i.e. politics) still below that, we have the idea that the very act of thinking being serves as a political action—not in the end as a form of knowledge that can be formulated in a judgement, but rather as a form of practice that aims at an intervention.

In order to make sense of this notion of philosophy as an acting intervention, the very notion of philosophical argumentation must be reformulated. The idea of philosophy consisting simply in profoundly clear arguments that are exchanged between rational agents, who have the wisdom and responsibility to accept good arguments and reject bad ones, is not necessarily completely set aside (after all Agamben is certainly providing arguments), but it is unseated from the throne of philosophical endeavour. The aim of philosophy is not necessarily to provide clear and distinct statements and sentences, which are argued to be true, with the aim of making the interlocutor accept the truth of the statements. Rather, the aim might equally be said to be to make the interlocutor start to think; to take him or her out of the habitual frame of reference in which he or she normally wanders about, and to force him or her to think anew. While this may be accomplished by arguments, it might equally well be achieved by a striking poem or a well-placed joke.

Since I am comparing Agamben to a tradition of French philosophy that emerged in the years following the Second World War, it can perhaps be helpful to distinguish his thought from some of the most general perceived notions about this tradition. One of the points this tradition has become famous for is the critique of metaphysics. A nice example, which will be relevant below, is Foucault's genealogical investigations, which aim to show how concepts and ideas that we have a tendency to sometimes take as universal truths in fact are the products of specific historical constellations and developments. A powerful reception of Foucault can be found in the work of Judith Butler, who in her early work *Gender Trouble* (Butler 1999) argues that any form of universalism is politically dubious, because the very formulation of a universal notion (of e.g. man, woman, race, culture)has a way of producing political inequalities; history tells us that every time we accept as universal certain notions of man and woman, the result has been the suppression of women. In this way robust ontological notions have a way of producing a reality that is unjust. In continuation of what I have argued above this has been one very popular way of introducing the direct link between an ontological frame and the concrete practices that take place within that frame; the very idea of being able to spell out such a frame can be seen as a way of repressing certain practices within the frame (for instance, in the way that the formulation of certain concepts of sexuality as essential to man and woman may lead to a repression of non-heterosexual gender-practices).

One problem with this approach, in comparison with Agamben's, is that it is somewhat limited with regard to the scope of ways in which ontological concepts can interact with a concrete practice. If the critique of ontological universalism becomes too forceful, it may lead us to overlook other ways in which the link between ontology and politics is absolutely crucial. One such instance can be seen in Agamben's book *Remnants of Auschwitz. The Witness and the Archive* (Agamben 1999b). In this work, Agamben argues that Auschwitz and the general experience of the European Jews at the hands of the Nazis shows us the fragility of any ontology of the human condition. What appears with all too terrible clarity in the concentration camp is the unbearable truth that whatever we may posit as the essence of man (that without which a man is no longer a man) can in fact be taken away from him even without killing him. Human beings can be treated in such ways that they loose speech, freedom, rationality and instead become empty shells. The *Muselmänner* of the camps—the term was especially used in Auschwitz—were exactly that: human beings who had their humanity taken away. They lost all traces of language, freedom, desire, rationality; they all died, but the crucial point is that they were living proof that the ontological structure of man, no matter how you formulate it, is ultimately amendable. Agamben's ethical point in the book is now that any ethics that cannot take the *Muselmann* into account is to be discarded. The more general ontological point is that there is a zone of indistinction between the ontological foundation of a field of practice and the actual practice that goes on in that field. There is no robust ontological foundation of what it means to be a human being; or rather, one can in fact point out what that foundation could be, but whatever is pointed out in such a gesture can also be taken away. The ontological foundation is therefore not a solid foundation, but rather a zone of blurred indistinctions. The difference between Agamben and someone like Butler (in *Gender Trouble*) should thus be clear. Where Butler—and with her many likeminded post-structuralists—would argue that the very idea of an ontology has certain dangerous essentialist tendencies, Agamben can instead stay true to the idea of ontology without the idea of a robust fundament, and that opens the possibility for an investigation into the zone where ontology and practice meet. Much of Agamben's philosophical work aims at the investigation of what goes on in the zones of indistinction that emerge wherever the ontology of our practices itself becomes part of that practice.

Genealogy

I mentioned above that Agamben's form of philosophical intervention is of a different kind than the one that is formulated in judgments and ideally exchanged between rational interlocutors. This has to do with his ambition of resisting the juridification of thought. In the words of two prominent commentators, he specifically wishes to resist 'reducing it to judgements about this and that, a weighing of pros and cons, a problem-solving technique' (Murray & Zartaloudis 2009, p.208). A good reason for this hesitation, and a nice way of understanding Agamben's genealogical project, is that the juridical form of thought itself has been produced by a particular history and by certain political forces—and not necessarily the ones we would normally expect. Juridified thinking has turned out to be both a very help tool in general, but that does not necessarily mean that philosophical reflection should be conducted exclusively in juridical terms—i.e. as a linguistic practice that aims at producing definitive statements.

Michel Foucault, whom Agamben considers his predecessor in the investigation into the genealogy of governmentality (Agamben 2011, p.xi), famously wrote about the development of penal practices in *Discipline and Punish* (Foucault 1995). In the years prior to the publication of that book, Foucault worked on the relation between juridical practice and truth. This theme was presented in the lecture series entitled 'Truth and juridical forms' that were held in 1973 at the Pontifical Catholic University of Rio de Janeiro. Here Foucault argues, first of all, that 'the subject of knowledge itself has a history; the relation of the subject to the object; or, more clearly, truth itself has a history' (Foucault 2002, p.2). Second, he argues that this history is one that has been dominated primarily by developments in juridical practice. Foucault shows how the practice of producing truth through reference to proof and observation, developed by the ancient Greeks for establishing legal guilt and innocence, were only subsequently adopted by the scientific practices so familiar to us today. He further shows how juridical practice has moved back and forth since those days, and with it our general thinking about truth.

With this in mind one can argue for Agamben's hesitation towards the juridification of thought, that the uncritical acceptance of one par-ticular (juridically founded) regime for producing truths should be avoided. There are other possible ways of working with thought than those that lend themselves to abstract calculations and supposedly definite and clear statements. A 'weaker' thought (to use a term proposed a different times by two of Agamben's other great sources of inspiration, Benjamin and Deleuze) i.e. a thought that indicates, suggests and implies rather than stating, concluding and proving may in certain instances be preferable. The notion of weak thought, however, is not one that I will pursue in great detail here. Instead, I will focus on the notion of genealogy, and hence on the Foucauldian legacy that Agamben has taken up.

In *Discipline and Punish* Foucault embarked on the study of the genealogy of governmentality. His earlier works were what he called 'archaeological studies', which briefly put means investigations into the unconscious rules that structure discursive formations at a certain time in history. The point of the archaeological method is that it can reveal how the rules and concepts that were readily available in previous periods can later on be forgotten, even though the structures they describe are still in place—this is precisely what it means to say that they are unconscious. The genealogical investigations aimed to unveil the transitions between such unconscious systems of rules. Thus, for example, *History of Madness* (Foucault 1964) can be seen as an archaeological investigation of the way in which madness was conceived in the 17th and 19th centuries, with the aim of showing how some of these structures still dominate our thinking about madness. The genealogical investigation in *Discipline and Punish*, on the other hand, seeks to understand the massive *changes* that went on in the practices of punishment in the 18th and 19th centuries. Famously, Foucault began the book detailing how, in 1757, Damien the regicide was tortured, having skin and flesh torn off with red-hot pincers, and ultimately killed by being pulled apart by horses. Immediately thereafter, he detailed how only 80 years later criminals were put in detention cells where they would lead lives of discipline and regulation to the minutest detail. What Foucault argued had taken place in those years of change was that a new regime of governance took hold in Western societies, one that not only extended to entirely new practices in the penal system, but also—and crucially—to the whole range of institutions we hold to be central to our societies: hospitals, schools, asylums, universities, etc. Here we find Foucault's famous reading of Bentham's idea of the panopticon prison, where the constant surveillance—or rather the feeling of being under constant surveillance—submits the inmates to a level of discipline that makes the wall of the prison almost superfluous.

What changes in this development, according to Foucault, is not simply an institution or a particular practice. What changes is the very frame of thought in which such institutions are formed. To use a key term for Foucault that is also very important for Agamben, we can say that the dispositive of power changes. Crucial for Agamben's understanding of the dispositive is that he discusses it in ontological terms, but the overall point of genealogical investigations is that they aim at the historicity of the fundamental frame of our practices; they target that which would seem to be universal and solid, but which turns out to be historical and changeable. Thus, for Agamben, it is the historicity of ontology that is in focus.

In this way a crucial strength of genealogical investigations is the ability to establish surprising connections and nonlinear causal relations in historical developments (the very linearity of history itself would merely be one such frame of thought, it would be part of one specific dispositive). We should allow ourselves to be surprised of the fact that certain developments within penal practice, and the birth of the prison, can be seen to have a profound impact on the ways in which we think about health, education, science, religion, etc. In Agamben's genealogical endeavours we find a keen interest and skill for excavating similar surprising links. A nice example is Agamben's contention that developments in early Christian theology have had a profound influence upon the ways in which we unconsciously think about governance today. I will deal with these investigations in the chapter on *The Kingdom and the Glory* (Agamben 2011) below. And similarly, in *State of Exception* (Agamben 2005a), we find the surprising idea that a concept of ancient Roman law, *iustitium*, that has either been completely forgotten or hopelessly misinterpreted in fact serves to describe the legal situation of the global war on terror and its aftermath.

That being said, an outline of the rest of this book can be provided. Chapter 1 goes into more depth with the technical aspects of Agamben's ontological considerations, especially focusing on the notion of potentiality. Chapter 2 takes on Agamben's still most important work, *Homo Sacer* from 1995, looking into the crucial concepts of bare life and sovereign power. Chapter 3 discusses *State of Exception*, with the explicit aim of correcting some of the unfortunate misperceptions that the work has been subjected to, probably because of the explosive political thematic it deals with. *State of Exception* famously discusses the legal situation of the years following 9/11 during a time when that legal reality was most pertinent for the public eye. Doing so, while being very critical of the dominant ideological perception of the war on terror, will inevitably lead to some harsh and often unjust criticisms being raised. I will try to show briefly how these criticisms are wrong and, more importantly, what the crucial and unfortunately much overlooked lesson from *State of Exception* really is. Chapter 4 takes on Agamben's work on economic theology mentioned above and epitomized in *The Kingdom and the Glory*. Here, we will learn how the discussions on the understanding of the Trinity in early Christian theology would come to shape the way we unwittingly think about power and government today. Chapter 5 looks into Agamben's less diagnostic and more normative work, for lack of a better word his idea of *emancipation*, which is centred on a special link Agamben establishes between messianism and profanation.

Chapter 1: Potential ontology

Agamben's ontology is centred on the notion of potentiality. His studies on potentiality are, for good reason, intricately linked to readings of Aristotle. I say for good reason, because Aristotle was the one who made the first crucial step in the philosophical theorizing of potentiality in the work that has since then been collected and named *Metaphysics* (Aristotle 1960). But Agamben's concept of potentiality is an enigmatic one. Even though his interest in Aristotle could make us think of him as an Aristotelian, his idea of a 'potentiality as such', a potentiality which 'gives itself to itself' (Agamben 1999a, p.184) seems to bring him out of contact with the specific Aristotelian way of thinking about potentiality. In Aristotelian thought potentiality (dynamis) is closely tied to actuality (energeia)—there is no way for potentiality to relate only to itself. Agamben is clearly arguing that his way of reading Aristotle is in fact closer to the truth of the text than most standard accounts, but it should be evident that his reading is controversial.

In order to properly understand Agamben's ontological thought, and especially his notion of potentiality, we should first of all take a look at its Aristotelian origin. I think it is evident that Agamben's way of treating the notion takes him beyond the Aristotelian framework—at least beyond the way Aristotle is usually understood. Agamben himself seems to be aware of this, as he argues that his interpretation of Aristotle focuses on sentences that have always been overlooked, misinterpreted or ignored by traditional Aristotelian scholars (Agamben 1998, p.45; Agamben 1999a, p.183). Hence the second, and crucial, step in the exposition of Agamben's notion of potentiality will be to pinpoint where his theory takes him away from the standard Aristotelian story.

Aristotle on potentiality

In Aristotle, potentiality (dynamis) always relates to a form of actualization (energeia). To be potential means to be a possible actualization. There are several ways in which these concepts can relate. In book Theta of the *Metaphysics*, Aristotle initiates his discussion of the terms by dividing powers (potentialities) into passive and active ones (Aristotle 1960, p.1046a). A thing can potentially have another form or be another thing altogether. In this way, wood can be cut to change its shape and in the end be made a chair or a table. A thing can also have the active power to change the form of another thing. In this way fire has the ability to burn wood and to turn it to dust.

Concerning persons, there are several things to be said about the Aristotelian categories of dynamis and energeia. First of all, persons possess both active and passive powers. As a child, a person can to some extend be regarded as a material in the same way as wood. It possesses the passive power of being able to learn. Through education a child can be formed into something that it would not otherwise be; it could for instance be taught carpentry. Prior to such education a child already has some rudimentary skills of carpentry (i.e., active powers); given a knife and a piece of wood most children will be able to cut the wood into some new form. Rough as it is, however, such forming still does not amount to (real) carpentry. But by having such a basic ability to deal with knives and wood, the child is potentially a real carpenter.

Aristotle, however, also considers a second kind of potentiality. This is the kind of potency that is found in a fully educated carpenter. An educated carpenter has fully actualized his original potential for learning carpentry, but this actuality (this fully actualized potential) is in itself yet another potential. This second potential is the carpenter's ability to form wood in a skilful manner—his ability to do carpentry. Having spent a fair amount of time learning the trade of carpentry, a person is free in a sense in which he was not before his training.

In Aristotelian potentiality, we find a project of freedom in the interplay of first and second potentiality. The point of this Aristotelian notion of potentiality can be further clarified by taking a look at Aristotle's discussion with the Megarians in *Metaphysics* Theta.

According to the Megarians, there is 'no power apart from its operation' (Aristotle 1960, p.1046b). Following this idea, a carpenter would only be a carpenter insofar as he is actually doing carpentry. In other words, according to the Megarians, the carpenter is only a carpenter when he is actually engaged in carpentry. Aristotle argues against this idea in that it makes it impossible to understand what it means to have an acquired ability: 'Hence, when a man ceases to practice his art and is supposed no longer to have it, how can he have acquired the art anew when he subsequently readily knows how to [do it]?' (Aristotle 1960, p.1047a). If a carpenter only knows how to be a carpenter when he is actively forming wood, and loses this knowledge when he stops, how can he suddenly regain it when he later on wishes to continue his work? Clearly that would impossible if we do not accept that potentiality of the second order is something that a person acquires—and is both able to actualize and refrain from actualizing—as long as he is in the possession of that potentiality.

From these arguments we can conclude that the kind of freedom that Aristotle indicates through his concept of potentiality is a concept of freedom as mastery. By undergoing the transition from first to second potentiality a person can learn to master an ability or a trade. But this transition is, of course, not limited to such matters. It could also be the kind of transition one undergoes in being initiated into a society, or in learning how to act in moral or political matters. The kind of freedom that is found in such mastery could be understood as the ability to dismantle the straightforward relation between potentiality and actualization. In such mastery we find the ability to suspend potentiality's full actualization. There is always something potential about second potentiality, even when it is actualized. This is what characterizes a master; he is able to adjust to the specific conditions under which he is working, he is never simply applying a rule or blindly actualizing his potential. He is always in command of an extra potential that can be called forth when the situation calls for it.

Agamben transcending Aristotle

It is this last feature of second potentiality that is of special interest to Agamben: the idea that potentiality is not exhausted in its own actualization. His target is the idea of potentiality that is 'carried over' as potentiality in being actualized. This brings him to a concept of potentiality as such, which is the notion of potentiality that is central to his thought. Potentiality as such is a potentiality that relates only to potentiality itself; it is a potentiality that is not merely a potential actualization; it is a potential potentiality. In coining such a term, however, Agamben is transcending Aristotle, or at least the way Aristotle is usually understood. By gaining an understanding of how this further step is supposed to work, we will get a view to the crucial feature of Agamben's ontology.

In order to get at such a pure potentiality, it seems evident that Agamben needs to downplay the role of first potentiality in getting at second potentiality. If the kind of potentiality that 'gives itself to itself' is something that can only be achieved through the actualization of some first potentiality, then there is always something actualized about this second kind of potentiality. This in turn would mean that it could never be pure. Therefore Agamben writes:

> There is a generic potentiality, and this is the one that is meant when we say, for example, that a child has the potential to know, or that he or she can potentially become the head of State. This generic sense is not the one that interests Aristotle.
>
> The potentiality that interests him is the one that belongs to someone who, for example, has knowledge or an ability (Agamben 1999a, p.191).

One could argue that by overlooking the necessary temporal precedence of first potentiality over second potentiality, Agamben is indeed stepping out of the Aristotelian line of thought. And since he is doing so with the aim of giving reasons for the intelligibility of a notion of potentiality where potentiality takes ontological priority over actuality—in the sense that one can think potentiality without subsuming it to some prior notion of actuality—therefore it is quite evident that there is at least some tension between the Aristotelian notion of potentiality and the Agambendian one. This is abundantly clear in a passage from *Metaphysics* Theta: 'It is evident that actuality is prior to potentiality. And I mean prior not only to the definite power which is said to be the source of change in something else or in some other aspect of the same thing, but to any source of motion or of rest generally' (Aristotle 1960, p.1047a). Immediately after this passage, however, Aristotle does in fact leave room for one specific kind of priority to potentiality over actuality: that of a particular kind of temporality. The wooden table, at which I am writing these pages, could not have become an actual wooden table, if it had not been a potential table first. In this sense the potentiality for something to come into being must necessarily precede the actual coming into being of that thing. Thus there is a kind of temporal priority of potentiality over actuality. However, this prior potentiality itself must immediately be subsumed to an actuality, because no matter how one conceives of the potential table, before it comes into actual being, it is only possible by being actual in some form or other—if there are no actual trees then there are no possible wooden chairs. This is a cornerstone of Aristotle's theory of the relation between potentiality and actuality. Thus, even where Aristotle admits that potentiality can have some priority with regard to actualization, he immediately retracts and argues that this form of priority is only thinkable under the assumption that this prior potentiality is again subsumed to a higher order of actuality (Aristotle 1960, p.1049b). And thus actuality remains ontologically prior to potentiality. As we will come to see, this is what Agamben alters with his rather special reading of Aristotle.

Before I go on to discuss this reading, it will be good to have a notion of how the Aristotelian conception can have profound political force in current philosophical debates. Here it will be worthwhile to consider the work of Martha Nussbaum, who, at times in conjunction with Amatya Sen, has proceeded from the Aristotelian considerations I expounded above. In the approach of Nussbaum and Sen, the second notion of potentiality discussed by Aristotle (i.e., the notion of potentiality that is involved, for instance, in having learned a trade such as carpentry) is usually termed *capacity* or *capability*.

To have a capacity exactly means to be able to actually do the thing one is capable of. If a young bashful man with no skill in carpentry were to say 'I can make a beautiful chair', it would in a certain sense be true. He could indeed make a beautiful chair, if he were to take the time to learn the necessary skills. But in the important sense it would of course be false, because he does not yet have the capacity to make a chair. He is precisely not actually capable of doing so.

In this way Nussbaum's account of Aristotelian thought brings about a crucial difference between mere logical possibility and actual capacities—a distinction that certainly is important in its own right, but which does not capture the specific point Agamben is making. The idea of the capabilities approach, founded by her and Sen, is to focus on the capabilities a person has in order to assess his or her 'ability to achieve various valuable functionings as a part of living' (Nussbaum & Sen 1993, p.30). This should be seen as a countermove to more common approaches within the social sciences that focus, for instance, on utility, opulence, negative freedom, and other concepts that can be reduced to formalisms. A good example is found in the study of constitutional law, where Nussbaum argues that rights formally guaranteed by the constitution are worthless if they are not also actualizable in the concrete life of the people living under that constitution (Nussbaum 2007, pp.6–7). In this way Nussbaum's Aristotelianism targets the idea that to have a capacity means to actually be able to do something. If I am formally free to seek my own version of the good life, but at the same time severely hindered due to my being subjected to institutional discrimination, then my formal freedom is not worth very much. *A capacity is an actualized state one is in, where one can actually actualize a certain potential.*

In this way of rendering the Aristotelian notion of potentiality, the crucial point of a genuine capacity is the idea of *actualization*. If one in fact cannot actualize one's potentiality, then the very notion of potentiality stops making sense. It becomes empty. While this is an important point in its own right, the point Agamben is making is in many ways the very opposite.

Just like Nussbaum, Agamben takes Aristotle's second notion of potentiality as a capacity as his starting point. But from there he leaves the standard interpretation behind and instead goes on to search for a concept of 'potentiality as such', as mentioned above. But taking the position opposed to Nussbaum, where the criterion for a genuine potentiality is its actualizability, the ultimate notion of potentiality, according to Agamben, is *impotentiality*. Seen from the more traditional Aristotelian point of view, and indeed from the point of view of common sense, this idea of potentiality as impotentiality is certainly counterintuitive. As a result of this, Agamben emphatically denies that Aristotle places actuality at a more fundamental ontological level than potentiality, something that seems to bring him in flagrant contradiction with most standard readings of Aristotle as well as the texts themselves.

In short, what Agamben does in his reading of Aristotle is to turn upside down the entire ontological hierarchy taken for granted by most forms of Aristotelianism. Nevertheless, Agamben insists on finding what he is looking for within the Aristotelian corpus. It should thus be no surprise that he is rather selective in his choice of passages from Aristotle's work, and it is hard not to think that it would be impossible to uphold the reading Agamben is conducting, if one were to engage with the entirety of texts that are available. At the very least it should be pointed out that his reading is controversial.

Agamben places particular emphasis on three passages from Theta. First of all, these two: 'Impotentiality is a privation contrary to potentiality. Thus all potentiality is impotentiality of the same and with respect to the same' (Aristotle 1047a quoted Agamben 1999a, p.183; Agamben 1998, p.45), and 'What is potential is capable of not being in actuality. What is potential can both be and not be, for the same is potential both to be and not to be' (Aristotle 1050b quoted Agamben 1999a, p.183; Agamben 1998, p.45). Agamben argues that in these two passages Aristotle himself is going beyond the standard conceived notion of Aristotelian capacity. His claim is that for Aristotle 'All potentiality is impotentiality of the same and with respect to the same' does not merely mean that to have a capacity is to also have a specific capacity of not actualizing one's capacity. Instead, he takes it to mean that potentiality *essentially* is impotentiality. The point is that one only finds the full force of a capacity in its ability to not come into actuality; it is not simply that potentiality means that which can both become actualized and not become actualized, it is rather that the ultimate truth of potentiality is *im*potentiality.

This idea can in fact be expressed quite nicely in the terms of the argument we saw Aristotle present against the Megarians above. If we can only make sense of the capacity for carpentry by accepting that it does not disappear when the carpenter is not engaged in carpentry, then it must be the case that what characterizes this capacity more than anything else is found where it is not actualized. What is crucial about the capacity for carpentry is something that must remain un-actualized—it is im-potentiality.

The crucial issue for these notions of impotentiality and potentiality not-to is thus how they stand in relation to actuality. If potentiality is a notion of something that is entirely without relation to reality, if it is merely an abstract notion of possibility, like the one we discussed above where any brash young man could say 'I can make a beautiful chair' (with the implied clause that he could if he were to undertake years of training in order to learn carpentry), then the notion of potentiality as impotentiality would be nonsensical, or worse irrelevant.

Agamben is quite aware of this. The crucial manoeuvre of his reading of Aristotle lies in the way he gives an answer to the question: how does potentiality retain any relation to actuality if it is essentially impotentiality? If potentiality is ultimately impotentiality, meaning that its essence consists of not coming into actuality, in what sense can potentiality then be said to have a relation to actualization? In answering this question, Agamben quotes what is evidently his favourite passage from *Metaphysics*:

> The answer Aristotle gives to this question is contained in two lines that, in their brevity, constitute and extraordinary testament to Aristotle's genius. In the philosophical tradition, however, Aristotle's statement has gone almost entirely unnoticed. Aristotle writes: 'A thing is said to be potential if, when the act

of which it is said to be potential is realized, there will be nothing impotential' (*esti de dynaton touto, hoi ean hyparxei hē energeia ou legetai ekhain tēn dynamēn, ouden estai adynaton*) (Agamben 1999a, p.183; see also Agamben 1998, p.45).

That these lines have gone unnoticed is due to the fact that they are mostly interpreted quite differently from the way Agamben sees them. Generally, they are simply understood to render a tautological statement, saying: 'Potentiality is that from which there results no impossibility when it is actualized'. This way of understanding the sentences is also very clear in many, if not most, translations of the text. Agamben's point is instead that the final clause of Aristotle's statement—i.e. 'there will be nothing impotential'—specifies a way in which potentiality, understood as essentially impotentiality, can actualize itself. In *Homo Sacer* he writes, 'What is potential can pass into actuality only at the point at which it sets aside its own potential not to be (its adynamia). To set impotentiality aside is not to destroy it but, on the contrary, to fulfil it, to turn potentiality back upon itself in order to give itself to itself' (Agamben 1998, p.46). In setting aside impotentiality, potentiality can become actualized, but this is not simply a cancellation of impotentiality, it is rather a way of carrying impotentiality over into actualization. It is a way of relating to itself as impotentiality without being completely pacified by it. In actualization, a potentiality sets aside that which is its own most essential characteristic, namely impotentiality. It should be clear that the operative term here is the notion of 'setting aside', which Agamben utilizes in order to achieve two things. First of all that potentiality retains some relation to impotentiality in becoming actualized, and second of all that this umbilical link between potentiality and impotentiality does not make the actualization of it impossible.

What Agamben means by 'setting aside' should thus be understood as a kind of suspension, an ontological way of pressing the pause button, rather than an outright negation. The outright negation would entail a too strict either-or, a vertical distinction between being and non-being. Instead, the setting aside should be understood in terms of the Paulinian *katargein*, a term Agamben is very fond of.

'Katargeo is a compound of argeo, which in turn derives from the adjective argos, meaning 'inoperative, not-at-work (a-ergos), inactive' (Agamben 2005b, p.95). In Paul, katargein is closely connected to the notion of law in the way that it designates liberation from the law; but according to Agamben's reading of the *Letter to the Romans* katargein means the liberation from the law as a way of fulfilling the law. In this way, katargein does not signify the enforcement of a suppression of the law; it rather means that the law is set aside and rendered inoperative. Katargein is a form of setting free, but instead of a strong negation it offers a weaker suspension.

The important point is that we should think of the 'setting aside' of impotentiality in a way that follows the trajectory laid out by the notion of katergein. In the actualization of impotentiality, it is left to itself or given to itself. Impotentiality is made to remain what it is, while potentiality turns into actuality. But because impotentiality in this way is merely suspended, it is not destroyed. It is still there, in a sense, ready to be activated once actuality 'needs a break.'

In this way Agamben's reading of Aristotle places actualization and potentiality on the same horizontal level. Pure potentiality is in truth impotentiality—it is the part of potentiality that must be with the carpenter, regardless whether he is engaged in carpentry or not, and for this reason it is itself never actualized. But this pure potentiality can be suspended and set aside in order for carpentry to be actualized, and in this way it is carried over into actualized carpentry in the form of suspension. Conversely actuality can be suspended and set aside without being destroyed, for example when the carpenter takes a break from his work but does not lose his skills in carpentry as a result. His actuality as carpenter is in this case precisely suspended rather than negated. But pure actuality, understood as actuality without any prior form of potentiality, is never actualized either, because there is always some potentiality present in the carpenter if only in the form of being suspended. Thus, neither potentiality nor actuality is superior to the other; both exist as extremes (of the same continuum) that can be suspended without disappearing as a result. In this way they are both at the same ontological level. Indeed, as these extremes they are fundamentally the same. They are both that which can be suspended in order for something else to take place, but they themselves are never fully actualized. 'At the limit, pure potentiality and pure actuality are indistinguishable' (Agamben 1998, p.47). It is by following this idea of a zone of indistinction between actuality and potentiality that Agamben establishes the link between ontology and his notion of sovereignty—a point to which I will return in the chapters below.

What Agamben does is to introduce a notion of potentiality quite different from the notion of potentiality found in more traditional readings of Aristotle. The notion of a capacity discussed by people like Nussbaum and Sen shifts focus onto the idea that in order to be a genuine capacity, a capacity must be actualizable in order for it to be understandable as a genuine capacity. Agamben turns the tables on this view by finding in the Aristotelian corpus the idea that the essence of potentiality is impotentiality. The only true potentiality is the one that brings about its own impotentiality.

The crucial point of this notion of potentiality is essentially impotentiality, however, is that helps Agamben introduce the notion of a zone of indistinction as a fundamental category of ontology. What we find at the bottom of Agamben's ontological edifice is not a clearly defined principle, nor is it a set of definitive conditions or judgments. Instead, what we have to confront as the most fundamental categories of being are notions that slide into their very opposite. As we shall see, this idea is not merely one that belongs to abstract ontological thought. Rather, the very thinking of such a zone of indistinction is as such a political thought.

Bartleby and pure potentiality

The Agambendian conclusion, that true potentiality is impotentiality, may certainly seem odd. At first it comes across as highly abstract, and to those who are inclined to believe that so-called common sense is a good guide in philosophical matters (I personally do not), it may be hard to see how such a notion of potentiality can be in any way helpful. Conversely, the Nussbaum/Sen notion that potentialities must be truly actualizable in order to count as genuine potentialities seems to be much more useful for investigations into social and political subjects. It even carries a critical edge that would seem appealing for critical projects that aim at uncovering, for instance, the hypocrisy in the celebration of certain formal rights that do not guarantee actual capacities.

Agamben's idea of potentiality as impotentiality, on the other hand, seems to be at first sight much less useful both for scientific and critical endeavours. It may be hard to see how such a notion can be helpful for furthering our understanding of political and social life; it may be very hard to see how such a notion can be useful for emancipatory practices and politics. Nevertheless, I take sides with Agamben here. The point of Agamben's notion of pure potentiality is that it opens the door to a new way of understanding freedom. One of the more illustrative ways in which he makes this point is through a reading of Herman Melville's 'Bartleby, The Scrivener' (Melville 2009) in 'Bartleby, or On contingency' (Agamben 1999a, pp.243–271).

In this novella, Bartleby is hired by a lawyer to serve as a copyist. At first Bartleby fulfils his function, but suddenly, one day when he is asked to compare a copy made by the lawyer's two other aides with the original, he simply says 'I would prefer not to' (Melville 2009, p.12). From that moment on the lawyer is unable to get any sort of positive response from Bartleby, at every request or demand Bartleby simply repeats his formula or some version of it. In the end, the lawyer finds it impossible to get rid of the scrivener—being told to leave, he simply replies 'I would prefer not', and so the lawyer moves his offices elsewhere leaving Bartleby in the old premises. That does not free him from trouble, however, as the new tenant seeks him out asking him to remove the annoying person he has left behind.

In Bartleby's formula 'I would prefer not to', Agamben finds a genuine expression of a pure potentiality, a potentiality that is essentially impotentiality, while it at the same time is an act. But this act is no ordinary act, since it is without object, without intention. Its true potential lies in its deliberate failure to constitute a move within any kind of language game. This act can be metaphorically described as a blank surface upon which it is impossible to leave any marks.

An important point in the narrative is identified by Agamben as the moment when the lawyer, in one of his attempts to scratch Bartleby's surface, tries to position him within the realm of the will. Bartleby is asked to go to the post office, replies 'I would prefer not to', is then asked in return 'You *will* not?', and redefines 'I *prefer* not' (Melville 2009, p.18). Agamben identifies here the effort to avoid any reliance upon the verb 'will'. The question for Bartleby is not whether he wants to or not, but rather whether he can—it is a question of potency or potentiality (Agamben 1999a, pp.253–4). Were Bartleby to have admitted to not wanting to go to the post office, he would have allowed for the lawyer to place a handle upon his otherwise blank surface. The lawyer would subsequently have been justified to ask 'why will you not?' and Bartleby would have been codified as someone with a reason, albeit one which he might prefer to keep to himself. This in turn would have created a duality between the surface of the action and the will behind it. In this way Bartleby would have been identifiable as any other person; the lawyer could have understood him as insubordinate, rebellious, or simply as wilful. According to Agamben this is exactly what Bartleby seeks to avoid. He is not simply refusing to take part in the symbolic order of the lawyer. He is enacting the impossibility of taking part in this order. This is why Agamben finds this particular narrative so attractive. Bartleby is in a most provocative and unnerving manner capable of his own impotentiality; he is therefore the paradigmatic image of human freedom.

Bartleby is the image of human freedom because he, through his capable inability to be placed within the register of the will, becomes impossible to identify as a subject. The will is—in other words— pointed out as the principle that makes coding and identification possible; that which is able to restore order to that which cannot be otherwise ordered (Agamben 1999a, p.254). In Bartleby, therefore, Agamben finds that there is nothing to be ordered and organized— there is only an abyss of potentiality (Agamben 1999a, p.254). This abyss, in turn, is nothing other than the unfounding foundation of human freedom. Agamben gives the following elucidation in 'On Potentiality':

[F]reedom is to be found in the abyss of potentiality. To be free
is not simply to have the power to do this or that thing, nor is it
simply to have the power to refuse to do this or that thing. To be
free is, in the sense we have seen, to be capable of one's own
impotentiality, to be in relation to one's own privation (Agamben
1999a, pp.194–5).

Freedom cannot be adequately understood if it is defined through
a dualism of positivity and negativity of the will. Freedom is not
simply the ability to do something that one could have been incapable of doing. Nor is it the ability to avoid having to do something
that one could have been forced into doing. In both of these cases,
freedom is measured though the number of options one has available. If someone has acquired an ability to do something that used
to be impossible, then he has increased the number of ways in which
he can act, but this does not make him free in the sense Agamben is
looking for. Likewise, if someone is able to reject being forced into
doing something, his range of possible actions increases, but it does
not make him free. This is because freedom here becomes reduced to
the freedom of choice. Making a choice confirms the legitimacy of
the options available at hand. To say 'I want this rather than that' is to
say that it makes sense to evaluate the different options against each
other; wanting something more than something else is to say that the
chosen object has a higher value that the rejected one. This in turn
entails the acceptance of a structure or system of values within which
the two can be evaluated against each other. Saying 'I want this rather
than that' identifies a set of values according to which one is will-
ing to make a choice. Every choice therefore entails the concession
'I am such a person that would make this kind of choice'; it entails
the acceptance of being placed within the context of that particular
choice; it confirms the ontology that is the condition for the possibility of choosing. This is the ontology where every person is identified
and coded through the choices that he makes. You are free to choose
whatever you want, but you are not free to exit the reality of choice.
Whatever you do, when you accept the notion of freedom as choice,
you are necessarily confined to the circumstances in which you are

given a choice. In other words, such a notion of freedom entails a necessary form of slavery.

What Agamben instead installs as the true concept of freedom is found in Bartleby's capability of his own incapability. The interplay of potency and impotence he calls 'the abyss of potentiality'. But more in line with the crucial concept we have been investigating so far, we could call it 'the zone of indistinction', located at the core of human activity. Bartleby's freedom consists of the ability to tap into the ultimate undecidability that governs human life.

Tiananmen

It should be noted that Agamben's idea of freedom is not simply some empty speculation undertaken for mere abstract philosophical reasons. In his *The Coming Community* Agamben sets out to describe this freedom that we have so far seen in the indistinction between potentiality and actuality, in the potentiality of impotentiality, in a series of short reflections. He begins by drawing upon classic philosophical, literary and religious texts, showing how Plato, Aristotle, Duns Scotus, Thomas Aquinas as well as Walser, Melville, Kafka, and Dostoyevsky, but also the Bible, the Talmud, and the Koran all tap into the power of this idea, when they express their most profound thoughts. The problem is that we have become accustomed to reading all of these texts in juridified ways (i.e. in ways that reduce them to preferred definitive statements about being or non-being, pro or con, good or bad). Agamben shows that we only have to look at them in a slightly different way, then we will be able to recognize the kind of freedom we have just seen him attribute to Bartleby. But he also shows that the freedom of impotentiality can be found in the most mundane circumstances. For instance, he takes up a commercial for *dim stockings* that ran in Paris movie theatres in the 1970s:

> It showed a group of young women dancing together. Anyone who watched even a few of its images, however distractedly, would have a hard time forgetting the special impression of synchrony and dissonance, of confusion and singularity, of commu-

> nication and estrangement that emanated from the bodies of the smiling dancers. This impression relied on a trick: Each dancer was filmed separately and later the single pieces were brought together over a single sound track. But that facile trick, that calculated asymmetry of the movement of long legs sheathed in the same inexpensive commodity, that slight disjunction between the gestures, wafted over the audience a promise of happiness unequivocally related to the human body (Agamben 1993, p.46).

Here, in a simple commercial, we see the usual images of the commodified (female) body. Of course we do. That is how commercials work. But we also find, according to Agamben, the visual experience of an un-graspable expression. A strip of film that works by commodifying the body suddenly turns out to make such commodification impossible, because one cannot ascribe an actual order to the dancing bodies. In this simple move, Agamben shows us how we can become aware of the reality of impotentiality in everyday life. It appears and it can be enacted—we simply have to learn how. In this way his overall philosophical project can be understood in a way that is characteristic of all good philosophy: as education. Agamben's philosophy educates us, in the way that it helps us see something we would not have been capable of seeing otherwise.

A further example of this is provided as he reaches the final reflection in *The Coming Community*, where he takes up the Chinese protests that ended in the massacre of Tiananmen Square.

> What was most striking about the demonstrations of the Chinese May was the relative absence of determinate contents in their demands (democracy and freedom are notions too generic and broadly defined to constitute the real object of a conflict, and the only concrete demand, the rehabilitation of Hu Yao-Bang, was immediately granted). This makes the violence of the State's reaction seem even more inexplicable (Agamben 1993, p.46).

According to Agamben, however, the extreme and apparent over reaction by the Chinese government might not be unintelligible after all. In a way there was a shrewdness to the brutality that should not be underestimated. It was as if the state knew precisely the point

Agamben is making with the idea of freedom as impotentiality. The very indeterminacy of the protests was what made them dangerous for the state as such, because in it the protests became something other than a mere struggle over the control of state power, and turned them into a struggle against the state itself. As he says:

> The novelty of the coming politics is that it will no longer be a struggle for the conquest or control of the State, but a struggle between the State and the non-State (humanity), an insurmountable disjunction between what-ever singularity and the State organization (Agamben 1993, p.85).

This does not mean that the coming politics is a struggle between civil society and state. On the contrary, civil society is nothing but society as it is already defined, structured and controlled by state power. What the protesters at Tiananmen Square instead expressed, if we are to believe Agamben, was the indistinct and indefinable potency of impotentiality. What terrified the Chinese authorities more than anything else was the fact that it seemed as if there were no demands to be met or rejected in the protests. The protests emerged merely as a blank slate, a surface that could not be scratched, as a promise of another way of life, one that is impossible to control and organize from the site of hierarchical state power.

Such is the promise of politics as Agamben conceives it at the most fundamental ontological level. As we shall see, however, the zone of indistinction does not merely serve as a promise for a future emancipatory politics. It is also, and crucially, a zone that can be entered into and utilized by state power. This point is part of the lesson we can learn from Agamben's still most famous book *Homo Sacer*.

Chapter 2: What is life? On *Homo Sacer*

Agamben's political philosophical project took shape with the publications under the headline 'Homo Sacer'—the first of which was *Homo Sacer. Sovereign Power and Bare Life* (Agamben 1998). In this instance we should pay attention to the subtitle of the work, as sovereign power and bare life are the two central terms in Agamben's diagnosis of the political condition of our time.

In the introduction to *Homo Sacer* Agamben draws upon the two distinct notions of life available to the ancient Greeks: zoé and bios. In ancient Greek, zoé signifies the simple fact that something is alive and not dead. Bios, on the other hand, describes life as taking a particular Form—e.g. the life of plants, animals and humans, but also, more interestingly, modern life, academic life, the life of a European carpenter or of a Persian king.

The question now is: what does it in fact mean to imagine a life that is completely bare? How can a life be lived, if it is pure zoé? Such a life, devoid of all form, is the kind of life Agamben seeks to understand in *Homo Sacer*. 'The protagonist of this book is bare life, that is, the life of *homo sacer* (sacred man), who *may be killed and yet not sacrificed*, and whose essential function in modern politics we intend to assert' (Agamben 1998, p.8).

This strange definition of the sacred man, who may be killed and yet not sacrificed, is not Agamben's invention. Rather, it is a juridical term found by Agamben in archaic Roman law. It is an obscure term that has no legal meaning or significance today. No one can be made into a sacred man—homo sacer—by a verdict of any legal body that functions today. Nevertheless, and this is where Agamben finds his inspiration in the genealogical investigations conducted by Michel Foucault, the idea of homo sacer is still with us. It functions as an unconscious background of our contemporary political lives. At times even, it is evident that we are still in a situation where human beings can be reduced to homines sacri, even though that is not the name we use for it today.

The other half of the subtitle of *Homo Sacer*, sovereign power, is equally important. When we talk about sovereignty today, we usually mean sovereign states, in the sense that in the international state system matters internal to particular states are not to be interfered with from without. As is well known, this notion of sovereignty—we could call it juridical sovereignty—is far from universally enforced, as it is often set aside because of so-called humanitarian interventions or because of wars. At other times we speak of internal sovereignty, in the sense e.g. that a people is sovereign in a democratic state (or the King is in a monarchy). Democracy here simply means sovereignty of the people. At one and the same time the people rule and are ruled—of course, the democratic states we know today all have some system for delegating sovereign power through elections and representations. The concept of sovereignty, discussed by Agamben, corresponds to neither the external concept of sovereign states nor to the internal concept of the sovereignty of the people. What he investigates is something that he would argue is fundamental and which in a way could be said to undercut both of these more commonly-used notions of sovereignty.

The more fundamental notion of sovereignty that Agamben is working with originates with a controversial thinker. He follows Carl Schmitt and the theological notion of sovereignty, which the German jurist and philosopher coined in the interwar years. The controversy extends from the fact that Schmitt was closely associated with Nazism in Germany in the 1930s. Agamben, of course, does not wish to follow Schmitt in following Hitler. Quite the contrary—the point he makes by taking up the theological notion of sovereignty is to warn us that the structure of sovereignty that was in place in the 1930s in Germany is still with us today and that it may have even more devastating consequences in the future. Before we can see what this means, however, we need to take a closer look at each of the concepts that are the focus of *Homo Sacer*.

Bare Life

Let us begin the exposition of Agamben's philosophical analysis of life by presenting the idea of life he wishes to defend. Having already noted his point of departure from two ancient Greek notions of life, zoé and bios—where zoé denotes the brute fact of life and bios signifies life that takes a particular form—the crucial Agambendian idea of life is relatively easy to explain. Agamben uses a neologism—'form-of-life'—to describe what he envisages as a potential emancipatory notion of life. The idea of this concept is to denote the impossibility of separating out zoé from bios. Form-of-life denotes the impossibility of separating out the brute fact of living from the specific form that life takes. In form-of-life, it is impossible to single out bare life as separated from the specific form life takes.

The idea behind insisting upon such a unity is found in Agamben's diagnosis that where life and its forms are separable, life is always at risk of being reduced to bare life. And as long as life is at the risk of being reduced to bare life, it is threatened by the state of exception. Here, Agamben often quotes Benjamin for the insight that the state of exception ('die Ausnahmezustand') is not exceptional (eine 'Ausnahme') but the rule. In the state of exception, bare life is the ultimate point of reference of political power. Life in this state is in essence only about survival. Here, all political rights can be revoked—all forms of life can be deemed invalid—in order to preserve bare life Such a situation is the condition for the possibility of political atrocities—a possibility which recent history seems to have confirmed all too often. The idea of a form-of-life, where no bare life can be identified or distinguished from its particular form, is thus the philosophical antidote which is needed in order to re-establish a true political freedom in the face of a permanent state of exception.

> A political life, that is, a life directed toward the idea of happiness and cohesive with a form-of-life, is thinkable only starting from the emancipation from such a division [between bare life and its particular form], with the irrevocable exodus from any sovereignty (Agamben 2000, p.8).

But so far, form-of-life is only a dream. What we have at present, what we are living, is a situation in which our lives are irrevocably caught in the sovereign ban, that is a situation where life is always potentially reducible to bare life. So we should take a closer look at this concept.

First of all, it is worth considering the effort it takes to even imagine a life that is nothing but bare life. What could such a life be? After all, whatever life is, it will normally tend to have some form at least. A life that is exclusively concerned with survival, and nothing else, is almost unimaginable. The point is that bare life does not naturally exist as such. It must be produced. Indeed, an important point for Agamben in *Homo Sacer* is that it takes considerable effort, and that special techniques are required, to produce bare life. Human life is normally never simply invested in survival. From the point of view of survival, human life normally deals with an incredible amount of pointless exercises: aesthetics, ethics, leisure, boredom, lethargic, snobbery, legality etc. To make all of these irrelevant for human life with one stroke could be said to require an act of genius.

It is this kind of cruel genius Agamben identifies in archaic Roman law in the concept of homo sacer. He quotes Pompeius Festus, who provides the definition:

> The sacred man is the one whom the people have judged on account of a crime. It is not permitted to sacrifice this man, yet he who kills him will not be condemned for homicide; in the first tribunitian law, in fact, it is noted that 'if someone kills the one who is sacred according to the plebiscite, it will not be considered homicide.' This is why it is customary for a bad or impure man to be called sacred (Agamben 1998, p.71).

The crucial point here is, of course, the link between bare life and sacred life Agamben identifies with this text. It seems clear from this description that homo sacer is indeed someone whose life has been reduced to bare life, because the law no longer protects his life. He can be killed without the killing being condemnable as murder. This would indeed seem to be enough to reduce one's life to bare life, because in that situation one would indeed have to always fear being killed. But the interesting thing is the identification of such a life with the sacred life. What does it mean that this life is sacred?

Agamben points out that homo sacer has been discussed to a significant extent in academic literature, but he feels unsatisfied by the results so far. This is first of all due to a notion of the sacred that has been almost universally accepted. Émile Benveniste, William Robertson, Sigmund Freud, George Bataille, Marcel Mauss, Émile Durkheim and many others have all subscribed to the notion of the *ambivalence* of the sacred. For Agamben this is a grave mistake (Agamben 1998, p.75ff). The ambivalence of the sacred goes to say that what we tend to view as holy (i.e. as the highest) is often also considered to be frightening and filthy (i.e. as the lowest). The ambivalence of the sacred can perhaps be said to describe something that has genuine psychological validity; it may be descriptively true that we experience this kind of ambivalence when we are confronted with things we take to be holy. However, Agamben first of all believes that this ambivalence in itself explains nothing, but rather is in need of an explanation, and second of all, with regard to the interpretation of homo sacer, he finds that the idea of ambivalence only serves to cloud our minds. It lures us into thinking that we have understood homo sacer simply by imagining this well-known feeling of ambivalence towards the sacred. We picture for our minds the great wonder and the great horror, we are used to feeling at one and the same time, when we imagine strange rituals, medicine men, totemic animals etc, and in the recognition of this feeling, we think we have understood. Agamben's point is that by doing so we do not explain the myth (of the holy), we rather indulge in it.

To escape the indulgence in the myth, we merely have to pay close attention to the text. What does the text explaining homo sacer actually say? Two things, and nothing more. First: to kill homo sacer is not a murder. Second: homo sacer cannot be sacrificed. For Agamben this means that the sacred man, homo sacer, is subjected to a double exclusion. He is excluded from human law, because that law does not protect him from being killed, and he is excluded from divine law, because he cannot be offered to the gods as a sacrifice—he is not worthy of being given to the gods.

To understand this duality we first of all have to notice that penal practices and sacrificial practices were intertwined in Roman law. Being subjected to punishment was at the same time a way of being purified. Agamben writes:

> The most ancient recorded forms of capital punishment (the terrible *poena cullei*, in which the condemned man, with his head covered in wolf skin, was put in a sack with serpents, a dog and a rooster, and then thrown into water, or defenestration from the Tarpean rock) are actually purification rites and not death penalty is in the modern sense (Agamben 1998, p.81).

In this way, in archaic Roman law, to be subjected to capital punishment meant to have your life invested with meaning—divine meaning. In capital punishment life was given a final form, it was introduced into divine law. This is what the condemned man, who is being made homo sacer, was being denied. His life was denied any frame of reference in which his life could take a specific form. Because of this Agamben identifies sacred life with bare life. Being sacrificed is to retroactively have one's life sanctified in such a way that it—even though one is now dead—counts as having had a specific meaning. It is this retroactive meaning that you are being denied, if you become homo sacer. For homo sacer, life is being made genuinely meaningless and death equally so. In this way, life is nothing but bare life.

We might still, however, feel that we lack an understanding of why this character is sacred, especially since emphasis has now been placed on the fact that he is excluded from divine law. The point is that whatever we do with a human life, even when we are treated in the most inhumane ways, we tend to necessarily interpret this life as receiving some meaning from the treatment. Victims of torture, for instance, are precisely interpreted as victims. This does not mean that it is nice to be tortured, but it means that in general a human life is a formed life, no matter how horribly it is treated. That is, insofar as it has not been made sacred. This point underscores the cruel genius involved in the term homo sacer; but it also enables us to understand more clearly what is meant by sacred here. There is an almost commonsensical understanding of the sacredness involved in the concept of homo sacer—namely, the one we know from the everyday saying that 'life is sacred'. What we tend to mean, when we say that life is sacred, is that whatever life may be, the mere fact that it is alive is something holy. But this is not at all an innocent idea.

The point is that the sacredness of life is far from something we should celebrate. Quite the opposite: sacredness of life is a much more dangerous concept than we would tend to think. We often seem to accept immediately that whatever the case, it is better to be alive than dead. While this idea may have some intuitive appeal, Agamben's point is that the political consequence of it is that we have developed a propensity to submit ourselves to sovereign power. In short, the lesson we should learn from Agamben's diagnosis of bare life is that we should be very worried whenever we are presented with arguments that draw their strength from the idea of the necessity of mere survival. What these arguments do to us is not only advise us on how to survive, but also and crucially to work towards a situation where we accept survival as the ultimate and perhaps even only realm of significance for a life. What we encounter here is a set of discourses that are not normally linked, ranging from medical practice and ethics, over ideas about gender roles, to security politics. What many of these discourses have in common is that they warn against the situation where, if we do not heed their advice, the survival of the species, the nation or the community is at risk—but what they all risk achieving is the reduction of our lives to bare lives.

The right to life is a fundamental idea in all declarations of human rights. But what kind of life is it that we are thus given the right to? This is Agamben's question. The problem is that it is not the right to live in a certain way or to give life a certain form. The primary right, according to declarations of human rights, tends to be the right to merely be alive. But having said that much, we have already admitted that it is bare life which is the ultimate point of reference for the law insofar as we follow the declarations on human rights. If we accept this much, we have already accepted too much. Agamben follows the German Jewish philosopher Hannah Arendt, who argued that the primary right must not be the right to life. Instead, the most fundamental right should be seen as the right to have rights. If we follow the idea of human rights, as we know them, to their foundation, we come to see that they presuppose an idea of life as bare life. This is the reduction Agamben finds problematic. If it is understood correctly, a human life can never be reduced to something merely factual. A human life is only understood correctly if it is understood with its possibilities in mind rather than the mere facts about its reality. The defining question about what a human being is is not the question about what it is, but rather the question about what it can do. In this way, it should be noted that Agamben's critique of the idea of human rights in no way can be squared with those, unfortunately relatively common, conservative critiques of human rights that argue that we should, instead of focusing on the human sphere and humanity, as we do when we talk of human rights, refocus on God. For Agamben the problem with human rights is not that there is too much humanity and too little God in them. Rather, the problem is that even human rights, immanent as they allegedly are, are still too invested with the notion of the sacred; namely, the sacredness of life as bare life.

An important point, therefore, in relation Agamben's analysis of homo sacer, is his understanding of religion. Here we have to take a short detour to another of Agamben's books: *Profanations* (Agamben 2007). In this book, in the chapter 'In Praise of Profanation', Agamben argues that religion should not, as it is often the case, be understood through the etymological meaning of *religare*, which means to bind. Although it is a commonly held belief, Agamben argues that there is nothing to prove that religare is in fact the etymological root of religion. Instead, he claims that religion originates in the term *relegere*, which 'indicates the stance of scrupulousness and attention that must be adopted in relations with the gods' (Agamben 2007, pp.74–5).

It may be hard to see why this should be of crucial importance, but when we consider that all religion deals with some notion of the transcendent, the point can be made clear. Religion understood in the sense of religare then becomes that which binds together a transcendent and an immanent realm. Understood in the sense of relegere, on the other hand, religion comes to mean the exact opposite. Here, religion is that which insists taking on a special attitude with regard to divine things; it is, in other words, that which insists on the essential difference between the divine and the profane. What makes this difference in the understanding of the word 'religion' important is that if one takes the notion of religion as religare at face value, then one is led to subscribe to the notion that there really was a transcendent realm in the first place, and crucially that it is through religion that the relation between the transcendent and the immanent can be established. But in the sense of relegere religion is first of all that which creates the separation between transcendent and immanent. As Agamben writes 'Religio, is not what unites men and gods but what ensures they remain distinct' (Agamben 2007, p.75).

To explicate this point, we can argue that religion, understood as that which binds the divine and the profane, is completely analogical to the situation where a biology teacher enters the classroom and announces that 'today we shall try to see if we can bind together Benjamin's head and body'. Such an announcement would probably make Benjamin rather nervous, and rightly so. Speaking of binding together only makes sense if the things that are to be bound have previously been separated. It is this original separation Agamben argues as the founding gesture of religion.

This means that Agamben has a very precise understanding of profanation—it is negligence. If religion originally means to uphold reverence for the separation between the things that are for the Gods and the things that are available to men, profanation means to be negligent towards that separation. In this way, to profane means to return a thing 'to the free use of the men' (Agamben 2007, p.73). This notion of free use is important, as we will come to see towards the end of this book. It is a central feature of Agamben's idea of political emancipation—his profane messianism.

This analysis of the concept of religion can also help us elaborate upon the notion of homo sacer. For this creature, life is no longer available for free use, because his life does no longer belong to the profane sphere. It is in line with this idea that we should understand the notion that to kill him is not a murder. Instead, the judgment condemning him to be homo sacer functions as the kind of ritual that rereads his life and places it in the sphere belonging to the gods.

However, the second part of the meaning of homo sacer seems to pose a difficulty in this reading, because as we have learned this character is also excluded from divine law.

One way of overcoming this difficulty would be to say that the reason why homo sacer cannot be sacrificed is that he already has been given to the gods. This would align very nicely with the idea of sacred life already touched upon, namely the idea of life is reduced to the brute fact of the distinction between life and death. When we say things like 'it is in the hands of God now' we mean something like 'from here on out there is really nothing more we can do.' At this point all that remains will often tend to be the simple either or entailed in the 'either it will live or it will die.' Here, there is nothing more to be formed, no more medical procedures to be undertaken to save the sickly child, no more water to be poured over the dried-out crops, no more precautions to be taken to ensure that the project will succeed.

In this sense, the sacred life is the life that is being given up from the point of view of human action; it is being left to itself; it is placed in the realm beyond any possible use. The problem with this reading is that it operates within a rather narrow understanding of the sacred, namely as that which is not available for free use by human beings. But the very definition of homo sacer Agamben has introduced seems to demand something more. As we might recall, homo sacer is not only excluded from the profane law but also from the divine. So, the problem is that we at one and the same time say about homo sacer that he is sacred and excluded from the divine realm. We say both that his life is in the hands of the gods, in the sense that it is no longer available for free use, and that his life is not for the gods, because he may not be sacrificed.

One way to manoeuvre this difficulty would be to say that the handing over of homo sacer's life from the profane to the divine realm comes with the added clause that this life is not received. Homo sacer is sacred because he is given to the gods but the gods do not accept the gift. In this way he is excluded from both the profane and the divine realms. Homo sacer is put somewhere in between—he is useless and not for use, but this uselessness does not bestow upon him the meaning which divine law offers. In fact, this is a perfectly sensible way of explaining the concept because there is one thing about homo sacer that necessarily hinders his complete transference into the transcendent realm, namely the fact that his body is still functioning. He still walks around in the immanent realm on his own two feet. This is the only thing that keeps him in this realm. He is dead to this world *except for the minimal fact that he is alive*. In this way homo sacer is a character who exhibits the precise characteristics of a zone of indistinction laid out above in the chapter on Agamben's ontology, only here it is the distinction between life and death which is ultimately blurred out. The important political point for Agamben is that the production of homo sacer must be understood as the development of a technique for creating a strange sphere such as this, in which life and death become indistinct and in which, therefore, bare life is directly available as an object of political power.

In this zone of indistinction, political power has the opportunity to extend the most radical control over life. When Agamben speaks of bio-power and bio-politics, he speaks of the form of politics that is enabled as a consequence of the establishment of this sphere. The meaning of this particular zone of indistinction will be further clarified once we have taken a closer look at the notion of sovereignty.

Sovereign Power

As I said above, Agamben follows Carl Schmitt when it comes to defining the notion of sovereignty. Probably the most famous sentence of Carl Schmitt's is the following: 'Sovereign is he who decides on the exception' (Schmitt 1985, p.5). In this way, sovereignty is inherently linked to the exception. We should notice the curious nature of this move. After all, a definition is in general supposed to give an understanding of what a thing normally is. We will come to see that the paradoxical nature of defining something through an exception comes into full force here. When it comes to the notion of sovereignty the norm *is* the exception; there is no real normality with regard to sovereignty; sovereignty is in essence out of the ordinary.

Consider the notion of juridical sovereignty and of democracy touched upon above. It was said that in a democracy the people are sovereign, in the sense that there is a relation of identity between the ruled and the rulers. The people rule and the people are ruled. This is a fundamental principle of how democracies work. The point about the theological notion of sovereignty, introduced by Carl Schmitt, with the notion that sovereignty is an exception, is that no matter how one wishes to structure this concept of public sovereignty, no matter which systems are set in place to uphold it and no matter how desperately we try to defend it, true sovereignty always appears as an exception to this rule. This is because any talk about democracy and public sovereignty must, if one pays close attention, in the end submit itself to a relative clause: the people are sovereign, *but only insofar as the state of exception is not in force.* No matter how well the bureaucratic machinery of a democratic state functions, it can always be set aside with reference to an exceptional set of circumstances—a natural catastrophe, a war, a terrorist attack or something similar. Here, the crucial point is that it is impossible in advance construe rules that define what the situation must be like in order for it to validate a state of exception In the end this has to be decided ad hoc as the situation unfolds (at least this is Schmitt's argument).

It is easy to confuse the conceptual elements that are in play here. I will, therefore, for the remainder of this book, make use of a terminological device that can be effective in establishing some clarity. When I speak about the factual set of circumstances (i.e. a war, a natural catastrophe or something similar) that by some will be argued to be a reason for setting aside the juridical norm, then I will use the term 'emergency'. When, on the other hand, I speak of the exceptions from the juridical norms that are introduced as a result, I will use the term 'exception'. This is not a universally accepted way of doing things, but I think it makes sense. It should be noted, however, that Schmitt himself, for instance, uses the term 'exception' in both of these cases (see e.g. Schmitt 1985, p.6).

The crucial point now is that it is very hard to define in advance what an emergency might be. An emergency has to be named an emergency in order for it to be a valid excuse for taking exceptional courses of action. The Schmittian point is that a *decision* has to be made. Someone has to take the decision to call the situation we are in 'an emergency' in order for it to be just that. The one, who is capable of making this decision will turn out to be the one who is sovereign. I said 'will turn out to be' because if we adhere strictly to this logic, it is impossible to tell in advance who is capable of doing this. Schmitt's work on constitutional law was directed at the problems involved in this difficulty. And in many ways his ambition—at least this is how Agamben understands him—was to secure some link between the law and the exception, no matter what the costs might be from a democratic or liberal point of view.

Take, for instance, the famous debate between Schmitt and the legal philosopher Hans Kelsen about the Weimar constitution and the crucial Article 48, in which it was stated that the president of the Reich has the power to set aside certain fundamental rights in the case of an emergency. Where Schmitt argued for a very wide interpretation of Article 48, stating that the state of exception, when announced by the president of the Reich, could mean the suspension of the entire legal order and not only the specific rights that are actually listed in Article 48 (Schmitt 2013, p.193), Kelsen argued against him that this would mean the reduction of the entire constitution to Article 48 (Kelsen 2008; McCormick 1997, p.144).

For our purposes the finer details of the discussion between Schmitt and Kelsen are not important, but the historical consequences of Article 48 should be known: it was a crucial legal tool that helped Hitler gain uninhibited power in Germany in the 1930s. As Agamben puts it in *State of Exception*, the Nazi regime should be considered legally as one long state of exception (Agamben 2005a, p.2). There are many details and historical complexities to this story, but I am unable to address them here.[1] The point of my very brief introduction to the context of Schmitt's thinking about the exception is merely intended to give some concrete background against which the highly theoretical discussions of exception and normality will be easier to grasp. But it is also helpful to have this background to the discussion in mind especially when one considers the critiques Agamben has

---

1   I have written about these in greater detail in my *The Metaphysics of Terror* (Ugilt 2012).

been subjected to. The point is that Agamben takes us somewhere quite different from the constitutional discussions indicated. This is often not taken into account when Agamben is criticized for following Schmitt. Agamben's point is not to take up Schmitt in order to learn something about how one should craft constitutional documents, nor is it his interest to learn something about the legality of current emergencies and exceptions. Agamben's project is philosophical through and through. What he finds interesting in Schmitt is the structure of his thinking about the exception. It is the way Schmitt introduces the relation of normality and exception into legal thinking that interests Agamben.

We should take care to note precisely what this means. It does not mean that Agamben merely wants to limit himself to completely abstract considerations of normality and exception. He most certainly wants his thinking to have relevance for the political and juridical reality we are in. But his way of thinking about this reality does not coincide with the line of thinking most jurists—or moral or legal philosophers—would expect. Agamben is not interested in establishing better legality within the current legal system; in this sense his thinking is anarchistic. Instead, he is interested in investigating the fundamental problems that attach to our current legal and political situation; the problems that one almost necessarily must set aside if one wants to discuss how the systems that are set up in this situation operate and should operate. This difference will lead many critics of Agamben to claim that his thinking is irrelevant for our current predicament. Conversely, Agamben would argue that if one does not deal with the problems he is identifying, one is set up to fail no matter how skilled one is in dealing with the functioning of the given political, moral and juridical systems.

The Sovereign Paradox

This brings us back to the question of how we should understand the Schmittian notion of sovereign exception. In *Homo Sacer*, Agamben introduces it as the notion of a paradox:

> The paradox of sovereignty consists in the fact the sovereign is, at the same time, outside and inside the juridical order. If the sovereign is truly the one to whom the juridical order grants the power of proclaiming a state of exception and, therefore, of suspending the order's own validity, then 'the sovereign stands outside the juridical order and, nevertheless, belongs to it, since it is up to him to decide if the constitution is to be suspended *in toto*' (Agamben 1998, p.15).

I have already mentioned the paradoxical structure of the Schmittian definition of sovereignty. Here, we receive a spatial metaphor to help elaborate this point. The very fact that we are speaking in terms of spatiality is not at all coincidental, as we will come to see below. But for now, we should concentrate on how this spatial metaphor helps us understand the sovereign paradox.

The sovereign is the one who can suspend the law. In this way he is outside. This 'outside', however, is not an outside in the sense of not having any relation to the law at all. After all, he has to have some relation to the law if he is to set it out of function. But the sovereign is not only in contact with the law in the sense that he is capable of suspending it; to Schmitt, the sovereign's capacity to suspend the law is in fact the foundation of the law. That is so because, in order for there to be law, the sovereign must not decide that the state of exception is in force. In this way, the sovereign's *in*decision is the ground of the state of normality.

This is the paradox of the sovereign's relation to the law. His only link to the law is that by which he is outside it. Sovereignty maintains the relation to the state of law in the way that it is included in the state of law as that which is excluded. Agamben further argues that this is crucial for our understanding of state power and of authority. Here, he puts himself in line with thinkers such as Gilles Deleuze, Felix Guattari, Michel Foucault and Maurice Blanchot. A common line of thought in all of these is the idea that power functions not by its capacity to exclude, but rather by its capacity to interiorize, to include.

Quite a lot of critical philosophy and critical political practices we see today tend to have the problem of exclusion as a main focus. It is debated and problematized, for instance, as to how women are excluded from positions of power, as to how minorities are excluded from certain institutions and social spheres, or more generally as to how the disenfranchised are kept outside. But, following Agamben, this is a mistaken approach. What Agamben tells us is that in the end there is no such thing as a complete exclusion. The crucial issue is rather—and always—that of inclusion. The problem the disenfranchised face is very often that they are included in the machinery of power and unable to get out; the problem lies with the specific way in which one is included.

Consider, for instance, the well-known debate about capitalism's exclusion of workers from economic and political power. What the conservative argument will say against this claim is that workers have the same opportunity to take part in the political process as everyone else; they have the same rights to vote and to take public office as capitalists do. And on the surface, at least in most current democratic states, the conservative argument will be right. However, instead of following this track, the argument put forward by Agamben and others (such as Deleuze and Guattari) would be that the problem of capitalism is not the exclusion of workers from representation or power, but rather the *inclusion* of labour power as the crucial commodity in the market. Having labour power as the crucial commodity in the market is to place the proletariat in a situation where they have nothing but their labour power to sell, and as the famous analysis of Marx shows, when you sell your labour power you never get the full value of your work. Capitalism works by extracting surplus value from workers. There is, of course, much more to be said about capitalism, labour power and political economy, but at present this point mainly serves to illustrate what is meant by holding inclusion to be the primary problem to be dealt with in critical political philosophy.

The point Agamben makes about sovereignty follows the trajectory of this spatial logic. Sovereignty should not be conceptualized as something that is wholly above and beyond the legal order. Instead, it should be understood as something that is included within it in the paradoxical sense of included exclusion. The interesting point Agamben makes in *Homo Sacer* is that there is same thing can be said about *bare life*. Homo sacer should not just to be understood as someone, who has been excluded from the legal order. Instead, he should be understood as the point where bare life is being included into the sovereign order. In a crucial passage Agamben writes:

> Here the structural analogy between the sovereign exception and *sacratio* shows its full sense. At the two extreme limits of the order, the sovereign and *homo sacer* present two symmetrical figures that have the same structure and are correlative: the sovereign is the one with respect to whom all men are potentially *homines sacri*, and *homo sacer* is the one with respect to whom all men act as sovereigns (Agamben 1998, p.84).

Both of these figures are to be understood through the theoretical and somewhat cumbersome notion of an included exclusion. Both of them should be understood as paradoxical limit concepts, but they should not for that reason be understood as merely theoretical concepts. Sovereignty is in fact functioning in our political world. This is becoming more and more apparent even today, perhaps we should say especially today. Think again of the el Masri case, and of the condemned at the Guantanamo Prison facility and the many secret prisons and camps that operate even now. Of course, there is a significant empirical discussion to be had about these matters, one that cannot be fully settled in these pages. All we can do here is to introduce Agamben's theoretical points such that hopefully they will enable us to illuminate the empirical debate.

Agamben's fundamental point in *Homo Sacer* is that the crucial function of sovereign power is slightly different from what Carl Schmitt proposed. Sovereign power does not merely consist of deciding—nor in non-deciding—on the state of exception. Rather, the fundamental gesture of sovereign power is that of including bare life into the legal order. By establishing bare life as the fundamental reference point of politics, we turn the notion of sovereignty and power discussed by Schmitt into reality.

This difference between Schmitt and Agamben can be made

clearer by considering the affinity Schmitt had for Thomas Hobbes (see e.g. Schmitt 2008). Both Schmitt and Hobbes see themselves as philosophical combatants of anarchy (i.e. the state in which there is no legal order whatsoever and in which no man can feel secure). And what both of these thinkers do to circumvent anarchy is to argue for the necessary establishment of an absolute hierarchical system of political power. Only a single hierarchical structure of power can guarantee the order and security Schmitt and Hobbes deem necessary for us to have a normally functioning political world. But by making anarchy the crucial danger which political power must confront, both thinkers implicitly make mere survival the ultimate point of reference of political power. In this way we find ourselves in the midst of bio-politics.

The fundamental question of sovereignty is the question of what it includes rather than excludes. This is crucial, because what Schmitt and Hobbes are trying to do is to exclude anarchy from the legal order, but what they achieve is to include bare life within it. The problems involved in this move can be made clear by considering another of Schmitt's works that also plays a crucial role for Agamben, *The Nomos of the Earth* (Schmitt 2003).

In *The Nomos of the Earth*, Schmitt argued for a fundamental theoretical link between order (in German: *Ordnung*) and spatialization (*Ortung*). The idea is that the crucial principle of *nomos* (i.e. of Law) is the drawing of boundaries:

> For the most concrete determination of what one calls international law, any medieval enumeration and listing of contents is illuminating even today, because appropriating land and founding cities always is associated with an initial measurement and distribution of usable soil, which produces a primary criterion embodying all subsequent criteria. [...]. All subsequent legal relations to the soil, originally divided among the appropriating tribe or people, and all institutions of the walled city or the new colony are determined by this primary criterion. Every ontonomous and ontological judgment derives from the land. For this reason, we will begin with land-appropriation as the primeval act in founding law (Schmitt 2003, p.45).

Law draws its strength and source from the stable ground of the Earth. Schmitt makes this point clear by referring to the fact that the sea is notorious for being without law. No one is capable of enforcing law at sea, because the sea cannot be appropriated in the way land can. In order to have law we need to first be able to draw a line marking out the boundaries within which the law is to be valid. Someone builds a fence and says: 'within this fence my word is law.'

Building a house, erecting a fence, making a home, and subsequently forming an alliance with other homes (in cities and in states) are ways in which we seek to assert our ability to control. Ultimately what we try to do when we appropriate land is to achieve what in Schmitt's catholic vocabulary would be the *katechon*, the suspension of the end of time or the *eschaton* (Schmitt 2003, pp.59–60). We build walls in the hope that what is on the inside may live forever.

According to Schmitt, this notion of katechon finds its best expression in Catholic theology, where the task of the Pope and the Church is to suspend the arrival of Antichrist. Katechon in this way does not make impossible the eschatological inevitability, but rather suspends it, gives it to itself in the sense of letting it remain at the point in time that never truly arrives: the end of time.

As mentioned above, Schmitt's thinking is very similar to that of Thomas Hobbes. For him, the most fundamental political problem is that of establishing order and controlling chaos. His greatest fear is that of total anarchy, because in the war of everyone against everyone life is, to quote Hobbes, 'solitary, poor, nasty, brutish, and short' (Hobbes 1997, p.VIII,9). But what Schmitt emphasizes is the point that no matter how great and powerful a state is, it will never be able to keep control of everything everywhere. Power can only function within a limited realm—and without power, there can be no law.

In the *Nomos of the Earth*, Schmitt argues that this means that a global legal order is impossible. No single power can make anarchy disappear everywhere, since it can only be done within the limits of certain borders. Accordingly, for Schmitt, it is absolutely necessary that there must be an 'outside' of legality—we can only be on the inside of a legal order if there is a definitive outside of it. This is why the classic European order, the *Jus Publicum Europaeum*, stands as the perfect example of a juridical order for Schmitt. In this order, the 'Lines of Amity'—that were formalized at the treaty of Cateau-Cambresis in 1559 and followed the tropic of cancer and Ferro Island meridian—marked a clear and distinct line determining what was inside and outside of the European legal order (Schmitt 2003, p.92). Beyond the lines, a legal state of nature was in place. For Schmitt the interesting point in this arrangement is the legal fact that conflicts that took place beyond the lines did not need to be continued on European soil. A conflict between France and Spain in the New World did not necessitate a conflict between France and Spain in Europe. According to Schmitt, this arrangement made sure not that war in Europe was made a thing of the past, but that wars of annihilation disappeared. In the classic European legal order, war was contained and peace a genuine possibility.

While Agamben finds Schmitt's thinking about the exception to be highly insightful, he cannot follow Schmitt on this account because Schmitt here seems to have forgotten the crucial point about the paradox of sovereignty. Schmitt's analysis of the European legal order rests on the notion that there can be made clear and distinct demarcations between order and chaos, but his very own concept of sovereignty is one that tells us that such a thing is impossible. The result of the sovereign's attempt to hold anarchy at bay and thereby to found and direct a legal order, as Schmitt envisaged it, is instead that a particular kind of anarchy—or rather a crucial feature of anarchy—becomes included in and central to the legal order. This feature is, of course, bare life.

Experimentation on life and the camp.

As I said above, it is not at all a natural thing to think of human life as bare life. Nor is it a natural thing to live one's life as a bare life. This is an important point, where Agamben differs from Schmitt. He does not accept the Hobbesian notion of a natural state of pure anarchy, because whatever a human life is, it is also always involved with something more than mere survival. Anarchy in the sense imagined by Hobbes and Schmitt is only an empty abstraction according to Agamben. Instead, following Agamben, it is necessary to actively do something to a human life in order to reduce it to bare life. But as we have seen, sovereign power needs bare life as a point of reference in order to function as sovereign power. This is what follows from Agamben's analysis that brings together the Schmittian notion of sovereignty with the notion of life entailed in the genealogy he draws from archaic Roman law. Therefore, Agamben's point is that Schmitt's contention that sovereign power works to keep anarchy outside of the legal order is false. There is a minimal point of anarchy retained within the legal order; namely that between the sovereign himself and his subjects. What sovereign power needs to do, in order to be and remain sovereign power, is to produce and uphold bare life as that which political power is all about. For this reason, the primordial gesture of sovereign power is not that of protecting bare life but rather that of producing it. Accordingly, an absolutely crucial practice of sovereign power is that of experimenting with ways in which bare life can be produced, upheld and managed. Agamben ends *Homo Sacer* with a brief review of certain practices he identifies as exemplary ways in which sovereign power achieves this.

The most effective way for a state power to conduct this kind of experimentation is the internment camp. Agamben's warning in *Homo Sacer* to the political bodies that exist in our current world is that we are confronted with a situation where the fundamental structure of politics is no longer the city, in which the enlightened citizens dwell, but rather the camp in which the homines sacri find themselves. The most famous internment camps are, of course, the Nazi concentration camps, and indeed—as mentioned—Agamben does devote a whole book to the investigation and discussion of this subject. Already in *Homo Sacer*, however, Agamben points out the obvious truth that the Germans were not the first to build concentration camps. The origin of the concentration camp is interesting for a crucial reason. Agamben writes:

> Historians debate whether the first camps to appear were in the *campos de concentraciones* created by the Spanish in Cuba in

> 1896 to suppress the popular insurrection of the colony, or the 'concentration camps' into which the English herded the Boers toward the start of the century. What matters here is that in both cases, a state of emergency linked to a colonial war is extended to an entire civil population. The camps are thus born not out of ordinary law (even less, as one might have supposed, from a transformation and development of criminal law) but out of the state of exception and martial law (Agamben 1998, pp.166–7).

The very idea of lumping people together in a camp emerged from the same exception that is the principle of sovereign power. Indeed, if we follow the logic expounded by Agamben, the production of camps and camp-like situations necessarily follows from sovereign power and the ever-enhancing security regimes that dominate international politics. Such a claim could sound alarmist, wherefore it is crucial to put it in the proper setting. It is clear that the ultimate reality of sovereign power, bare life and the concentration camps are all extremities. The concepts investigated in Agamben's *Homo Sacer* are all limit concepts. But the problem Agamben identifies is that these limit concepts are not easily kept the greatest distance from our everyday lives. This is so because they share the ontological structure of in-distinctions; they are structured as included exclusions. Therefore, we cannot simply place them in a clear and distinct 'outside' from the point of view of normality. Instead, they have a tendency to seep into our ordinary forms of political existence.

Auschwitz was extreme, no doubt. But the structures of power that made Auschwitz possible are still in place, and they have not grown any weaker over the last 70 years. What we see today, unfortunately, is a proliferation of juridical and political phenomena and situations in which the exception is becoming the rule. I have already mentioned some of the more spectacular instances in which this is relatively clear (the el Masri case, Guantánamo Bay, the Abu Ghraib prison, refugee internment camps), but it is interesting to note that Agamben also takes up a few other examples—some of them surprising. He especially brings attention to the many different ways in which medical science dissects, researches and manages bare life.

> Paul Rabinow refers to the case of Wilson, the biochemist who
> decided to make his own body and life into a research and exper-
> imentation laboratory upon discovering that he suffered from
> leukaemia. Since he is accountable only to himself, the barriers
> between ethics and law disappear; scientific research can freely
> and fully coincide with biography. His body is no longer private,
> since it has been transformed into a laboratory; but neither is
> it public, since only insofar as it is his own body can he trans-
> gress the limits that morality and law put on experimentation
> (Agamben 1998, p.186).

Agamben here identifies a bios that is so concentrated on its own
zoé that it becomes indistinguishable from it. Clearly this scientist
is freely entertaining this indistinction, and for that reason it is of
course much less morally problematic than is, for instance, the fate
of el Masri. But their ontological structures are similar, and in the end
the crucial problem here is not a moral one. It is the very structure of
politics that emerge with the possibility of these cases that interests
Agamben. Furthermore, it takes very little effort to remove the
freedom of choice from the equation:

> We enter the hospital room where the body of Karen Quinlan
> or the overcomatose person is lying, or where the neomort is
> waiting for his organs to be transplanted. Here biological life—
> which the machines are keeping functional by artificial respira-
> tion, pumping blood into the arteries, and regulating the blood
> temperature—has been entirely separated from the form of life
> that bore the name Karen Quinlan: here life becomes (or at least
> seems to become) pure zoé (Agamben 1998, p.186).

Agamben admits that his examples are extreme and that it may
seem unfair to put them together. After all, what do the attempts to
save the life of a person via an organ transplant have to do with concentration camps? At this point it is absolutely crucial to suspend
moral judgement. The point is not moral condemnation. Instead, the
point is that there is a specific structure to political power over life
and death, and that this structure repeats itself in these examples and
so many others. Agamben is warning us that we should not take this

repetition lightly. But that means understanding it in the proper political setting. The crucial point of Agamben's analysis of the relation between bare life and sovereign power is not that we should feel morally outraged when one person is reduced to bare life, nor is it that we should fear being reduced to it ourselves. Rather, the crucial point is political. As long as we live in the political world, where the link between bare life and sovereign power in the final instance will dominate the organization of our lives, then we cannot in any way be seen as free in any meaningful political sense. This is what it means to be caught in the sovereign ban.

In the next chapter on *State of Exception*, I will go a bit deeper into the problematic structure of sovereign power. In that book, we see some crucial modifications to the theory of sovereignty put forward by Agamben in *Homo Sacer*.

Chapter 3: Political theology. On *State of Exception*

In the previous chapter, we saw how Agamben draws upon Schmitt in order to understand the structure of sovereign power. We have also seen how Agamben clearly distinguishes himself from Schmitt, especially with regard to the attempts of sovereign power to establish and secure a legal order through the mechanism of spatial demarcations. As he says:

> The link between localization (*Ortung*) and ordering (*Ordnung*) constitutive of the '*nomos* of the earth' is therefore even more complex than Schmitt maintains and, at its centre, contains a fundamental ambiguity, an unlocalizable zone of indistinction or exception that, in the last analysis, necessarily acts against it as a principle of its infinite dislocation (Agamben 1998, pp.19–20).

This means that Agamben, as mentioned, cannot follow Schmitt in the Hobbesian argument for a strong centralized state power, which should guarantee the safety of the people. Instead, his point is that because Schmitt is right in his analysis of *what* sovereign power is, therefore we should be worried about the consequences of an uncontrolled sovereign power. In *Homo Sacer* Agamben is warning us against the effects sovereign power has on life, namely that it functions by integrating bare life as the focal point of the legal order.

In *State of Exception* Agamben changes his analysis to a certain degree. This is crucial for two reasons. First, Agamben is certainly not the only one who has argued that it is relevant to learn from and warn against the Schmittian notion of sovereignty in the current situation of the war on terror (see e.g. Gross & Ní Aoláin 2006; Scheuerman 2006). Second, because many of these analyses have been brushed aside by those one might call the 'critics of the critics' as alarmist or even conspiracy-theoretical musings (see e.g. Vermeule 2005), the very fact that Agamben takes us somewhere other than the standard critique of the Schmittian danger in the exercise of power in the global war on terror should heighten our attention. Unfortunately, *State of Exception* is usually read as if it simply continued the trajectory developed in *Homo Sacer* without modification. This means that the central point of the book tends to get lost. In this chapter, I will therefore focus on bringing out the particular facet of *State of Exception* that marks a crucial step away from the Schmittian paradigm laid out in *Homo Sacer.*

Schmitt and the dictatorship model

The idea that there is a Schmittian element to the legal paradigm of the war on terror is certainly not new. It has been the topic of intense discussion among legal scholars, philosophers and others since the attacks on 9/11. In general the debate consists of two camps. On the one hand, we have those who see in the legal response to 9/11 a dangerous development, which carries with it borderline totalitarianism in the midst of so-called liberal democracy. Here, the belief is that Schmitt's dark shadow hovers over us, because of the actions of democracies in the war on terror. And on the other hand, we have those who argue that these worries are wildly overstated, either because the changes made to fundamental aspects of the rule of law are argued to be inconsequential, or because it is argued to be necessary sometimes to sacrifice certain liberties in order to defend liberal democracy as such. Here, the argument is in other words either that Carl Schmitt's dark shadow does not hover over us at all, or that the shadow is indeed looming but that it is an unavoidable part of the struggle to preserve liberal democracy in the long run.

While the more polemical of Agamben's arguments, such as the one I indicated about the analogy between contemporary bio-political strategies and the Nazi Regime, could seem to make him fit well in the first position in this theoretical landscape, I believe that anyone, who has read *State of Exception* from cover to cover will find that it is really the *lack* of polemics of that sort that is the real surprise of the book. The greater part of the argument consists of what to many theoreticians and critics of the current global juridico-political regime must seem a rather tedious discussion of institutions of Roman law. My point here is that the 'tedious' discussions of Roman law are Agamben's most interesting analyses in the work. Here, he presents a theoretical model for the state of exception, and in effect for the state of normality, which is very different from the usual conception.

The central part of Agamben's argument in *State of Exception* is a critique of an assumption that is shared by *all* positions in the debate I sketched above. This is the assumption of what I would call the dictatorship-model. This point will become clearer with a short digression on Roman law and the juridical notion of dictatorship entailed within it.

Dictatorship should not be understood as just another word for tyranny or authoritarianism. Rather, the concept has a very specific meaning in Roman law. In the Roman Republic, dictatorship was a very specific juridical mechanism for dealing with emergencies. In the normal situation of the Republic the highest magistrates were the consuls, who possessed much of what we today would recognize as executive power, except for the fact that there were always *two* consuls. In this way the Roman Republic had a mechanism for keeping executive power in check inserted at the very top of the political system. In the normal situation no one magistrate was able to take too much power, precisely because there were two of the highest magistrates. While that system was an effective way of keeping power in check, a common argument (indeed one that is very recognizable in the current intellectual climate) would hold that it was a problem in case an emergency should arise. If an invading army advanced upon Rome, it would seem that there was no time to have two supreme magistrates come to an agreement; what was called for in that situation was for action to be swift and decisive.

In this situation dictatorship could come into play. It provided a model for dealing with emergencies that since then—consciously or unconsciously—has been part of the way most states deal with emergencies. Basically, a new highest level of executive political power was introduced, namely the dictator, who would have vast powers for summoning soldiers and of waging war.

The basic assumption that unites (almost) all positions in the current debate on the state of exception in general, and the war on terror in particular, is the assumption that exceptional measures equal a concentration of power like the one found in Roman dictatorship. The assumption is that exceptional legislation leads to the executive's, military's or police's powers enhancing. The debate then usually focuses on the normative value of such a concentration of power. There are those who argue that it is unfortunate, but necessary; there are those who argue that it is simply necessary; there are those who argue that it is not necessary at all; and there are those who argue that the perceived necessity of these exceptional measures is nothing but an ideological construct.

If we should place Agamben in any of these categories, it would be most prudent to put him in one of the latter two, but in truth that would not be an adequate representation of *State of Exception* at all, because the primary aim and interest of the book undercuts the basic assumption shared by all the listed positions—namely the assumption entailed in the dictatorship model. For Agamben, the model of dictatorship and the assumption that a concentration of power is a natural element of a state of exception is simply wrong; in his analysis the state of exception is descriptively—not only normatively—different from a dictatorship. To use Agamben's own terms, the state of exception we are witnessing today is not a pleromatic state of law, it is rather a kenomatic state, which is to say that the state of exception is an emptying of the law rather than a condensation of it (Agamben 2005a, p.48).

Given that it is an almost universal assumption to think of the state of exception in terms of the dictatorship model, the first thing Agamben has to do, to make his point, is to come up with an alternative model.

Iustitium rather than dictatorship

Once we have realized that dictatorship should not be used as a generic term for non-democratic authoritarian rule, but rather as a specific term that originates in the Roman law, then we should also realize that other forms of legal mechanisms could be imagined. Agamben does not have to look very far to find an example of another legal mechanism that works in a completely different way. He finds it in another concept from Roman law: *iustitium*.

'The term iustitium […] literally means "standstill" or "suspension of the law"' (Agamben 2005a, p.41). Where the dictatorship was meant to concentrate all power of the republic in the hands of one man, iustitium rather called for all magistrates to enact their imperium, without constraint from the law. And not only that, it also meant that all the ex-dictators, ex-consuls and ex-censors should act as if they were again in possession of their imperium (Agamben 2005a, p.44). Even ordinary citizens were to act as if they were magistrates. Agamben uses the example of Scipio Nasica to illustrate the point of iustitium. In 133BC iustitium had been announced by the senate because of the actions of tribune Tiberius Gracchus, but the consuls refused to act against him. Nasica, who was then a private citizen, called out 'He who wishes that the state be safe, let him follow me' and killed Gracchus (Agamben 2005a, p.44). About this act, Cicero later said 'Nascia acted as if he were a Consul' (Agamben 2005a, p.49). Following Agamben, this is important. Iustitium is the state of the law in which the 'as if' becomes the rule. It is a stoppage of law that does not entail a pure anarchy, in the sense of absence, but rather a state of law where the law is still valid but not in effect.

The difference between dictatorship and iustitium should thus be clear. When the dictatorship was in operation a new seat of power emerged in Rome, a seat of power that concentrated almost all power in the republic. Nothing of the sort took place in iustitium: 'On the contrary, in the iustitium […], there is no creation of a new magistracy; the unlimited power enjoyed de facto by the existent magistrates *iusticio indicto* [the *iustitium* having been declared] results not from their being invested with a dictatorial *imperium*, but from the suspension of the laws that restricted their actions' (Agamben 2005a, p.47). In this way the iustitium model challenges the crucial idea of dictatorship: it is not at all given that the natural way of responding to emergencies is found in the concentration of legal power in one person. A better way of understanding what is actually going on in emergency legislation would often be to see it as a dissipation of such power. This way of thinking about the state of exception will become clear once we consider the crucial problem that the Romans experienced with the legal institution of iustitium.

The problem was what legal sense one should make of the acts that were undertaken under the state of iustitium. These actions could not be said to break the law, because in iustitium the law does not forbid anything. And they could not be said to uphold the law either, because there was no legal rule to follow. What legal sense can one give to acts undertaken in a legal vacuum? Agamben gives a suggestion:

> If we wanted at all cost to give a name to a human action performed under conditions of anomie, we might say that he who acts during the iustitium neither executes nor transgresses the law, but in-executes it (Agamben 2005a, p.50).

In the normal situation of law, all actions can be said to have some straightforwardly meaningful legal sense. Actions can be lawful or illegal, or they can be legislative acts of creating law, and executive acts of applying law (Agamben 2005a, p.50). But the acts undertaken in iustitium are none of these. In the eyes of the law they do nothing other than enact the very lack of law, which is in place in iustitium. These acts can of course all be said to be the actual doing of something. Scipio Nasica actually killed Gracchus, but in a strictly legal sense it would be wrong to say that it was a murder, since the rule determining certain acts as murder was not in function. On the other hand, it would also be wrong to say that it was not a murder, since the very same rule, which should have been in place to proclaim Nasica guilty, should also have been in place to proclaim his innocence. Instead, Nasica's act is best understood as the enactment of the suspension of a rule (an in-execution of the rule) that could distinguish murders from other acts of killing. Nasica's act could in a sense be described as a non-murder.

Crucially, this means that Nasica's act cannot simply be said to be a case of anarchy. The state of exception is not simply a state of nature, where no-one is bound by any law or power. Instead, acts in the state of exception are undertaken in the very peculiar time of the suspension of law. There is a law, in virtue of which the act could be given a specific legal sense, only this law is not in function. Thus, when it is said that the act is one that enacts the absence of a rule that distinguishes murder from other killings, it should be emphasized that this is absence in the form of potentiality. That there is no rule in place through which Nasica's act has legal meaning does not simply mean that the law is missing in an absolute sense—it means that the act has the legal sense that there could have been a law in force which would have made sense of the act. The law is reduced to the state of being as-if-it-were-a-law. In this way it is the in-execution or the in-actment of the law. When Agamben uses iustitium as a philosophical model for the conception of modern states of exception, it is a similar form of legal emptiness-as-potentiality he seeks to explicate.

What Agamben's observations about the state of exception tell us is that the clear-cut Schmittian distinction between anarchy and law is too simple. There is no clear distinction between the inside and the outside of the law. Outside the realm of the law in its state of actuality (i.e. in its state of being in force as a law), we find the very same law only in its state of being a merely potential law. When we approach the boundaries of the law, we do not find ourselves a lawless state of nature; instead we find ourselves in a zone of indistinction between law and anarchy.

Having said this much we should now be able to see the differences of the perspectives Agamben lays out in *Homo Sacer* and in *State of Exception*. In *Homo Sacer* we get a largely Schmittian analysis of sovereign power. Here, the power to decide on the exception is equated with the sovereign paradox, and Agamben's analysis takes us to the point where this power becomes identified with the capacity to include bare life within the realm of law. Although already in *Homo Sacer* Agamben tells us to notice how the analysis Schmitt undertakes must in the end undercut Schmitt's ambitions for the notion of sovereignty, it is not until his work in *State of Exception* that we have the full extent of this point. Here, it is not only a matter of investigating the consequences of the Schmittian notion of sovereignty, but rather asking if it is a meaningful concept at all. By supplanting the notion of dictatorship inherent in the Schmittian idea of sovereignty with a notion of iustitium, Agamben gives us an entirely different picture of the notions of political and juridical power.

Benjamin not Schmitt

Having established that it is certainly possible to imagine the state of exception as something different from a form of dictatorship, Agamben still needs to make an argument for the point that what we are facing with the modern state of exception is something that resembles an iustitium rather than a dictatorship.

One obvious way of investigating this question would be to read the legal documents that spell out what is to be done in case of emergencies in various polities over time. Agamben briefly takes this approach in the first chapter of the book 'The State of Exception as a Paradigm of Government', in which he includes a short history of the French *état de siege fictif*, the German *Ausnahmezustand*, the English *martial law*, among others.

In the end, however, Agamben must take a different approach than a mere empirical study of historical juridical facts. His point is not that the kind of empirical juridical studies undertaken by many legal and historical scholars are superfluous, but rather that there are theoretical assumptions to those kinds of studies that are very often not questioned and that may obfuscate completely the subject matter at hand. To be concrete, if the dictatorship model has become an implicit assumption about our legal and political affairs, then we cannot expect that the legal documents that deal with emergencies and exceptions should in any way contradict the model. After all, those documents have been produced in terms of the very same frame of mind that has dominated the history of our legal and political thinking. Agamben's introduction of the way of thinking about exceptions that takes as its point of departure iustitium instead of dictatorship has as its aim the radical reconfiguration of the way in which we interpret those legal documents. Therefore, a simple empirical study of those legal documents will not do. What must be undertaken instead is first of all a philosophical discussion about the feasibility of the notion of dictatorship as such.

Agamben undertakes this discussion by working through an imaginary—or almost imaginary—debate between Walter Benjamin and Carl Schmitt. This debate is also interesting for Agamben for reasons of the historical discussion on the development of political philosophy in the 20th century. What he wishes to show is that there was in fact a crucial and overlooked debate going on between Schmitt and Benjamin on sovereignty and exception throughout the early part of the 20th century—and that theoretically they were much closer than one tends to think given their very divergent political stances.

Agamben argues that Benjamin's early essay *The Critique of Violence* (Benjamin 1999) should be seen as the point of departure for Schmitt's work in *Political Theology* (Schmitt 1985). This is in fact a striking claim, because if we take it seriously it means that Schmitt's 'Sovereign is the one who decides on the exception' means something quite different than is usually assumed. The way it is usually interpreted, this notion of sovereignty says something about what the sovereign can do with regard to the state of normalcy; namely to set it aside and enact a state of exception. But what Benjamin does in *Critique of Violence* is to argue that there is a kind of violence that escapes the law—an anomic form of violence that neither serves to preserve law nor to create it. For Schmitt such a form of violence can only be a form of anarchy, but for Benjamin it is something quite different. It is an idea of a revolution that does not merely aim at a capturing of the state and its institutions of regulated violence, but rather at liberation from the very idea of institutions of regulated violence and the dialectic of law-preserving and law-creating violence (Benjamin calls this 'divine violence').

Setting the debate between Schmitt and Benjamin on these terms is to say that the debate takes on a wholly different character than it would have if it were conducted from the viewpoint of the state of normalcy. The question is not whether the sovereign is capable of setting normalcy out of order (Benjamin, Schmitt and Agamben all agree here), but rather if the sovereign is capable of controlling the exception. Agamben puts the point as follows:

> The theory of sovereignty that Schmitt develops in his *Political Theology* can be read as a precise response to Benjamin's essay. While the strategy of 'Critique of Violence' was aimed at ensuring the existence of a pure and anomic violence, Schmitt instead seeks to lead such a violence back to a juridical context. The state of exception is the space in which he tries to capture Benjamin's idea of a pure violence and to inscribe anomie within the very body of the nomos (Agamben 2005a, p. 54).

So when Schmitt argues that the sovereign is the one who decides on the exception, in this view, he is talking about the decision with regard to exceptional violence rather than the decision with regard to the normality of law. In Agamben's reading Schmitt does not seek to make sure that the sovereign can always suspend normality, but rather that it can always control the exception that is introduced by the suspension of normality. This sets him up for a Benjaminian counterargument, which Agamben finds in the book on *The Origin of German Tragic Drama* (Benjamin 2003). It may be surprising that a book on an aesthetic subject should have something serious to say about the issue of sovereignty, but we should notice that there is a clear point of convergence between Schmitt's idea of sovereignty and German tragic drama. Both originate in the baroque.

In *Nomos of the Earth* Schmitt remarks it was not until the advent of the baroque that the state formed in the way we know it today (Schmitt 2003, p.145). Before this time, before the peace of Westphalia, it does not really make sense to speak of states in the modern sense with clearly defined persons of competence and institutions of power. Before this time, a sovereign in the Schmittian sense—where one person could be given the competence of being able to decide on the state of exception—could not be imagined. Likewise, the German tragic drama Benjamin is describing, has its historical origin in the baroque. Furthermore, as Benjamin argues, the theme of sovereignty is crucial for any understanding of classic German tragic drama (Benjamin 2003, p.65ff.). What Benjamin notices from his studies of the dramatic interpretations of sovereignty is a crucial deficiency in the very idea of baroque sovereignty. We could say that the German tragic drama presented an important theoretical reflection on a central notion of baroque statehood—a reflection that is that much more interesting because it was formulated at the time of the invention of this form of statehood. Benjamin writes:

> The antithesis between the power of the ruler and his capacity to rule led to a feature peculiar to the *Trauerspiel* which is, however, only apparently a generic feature and which can be illuminated only against the background of the theory of sovereignty. This is the indecisiveness of the tyrant. The prince, who is responsible for making the decision to proclaim the state of exception, reveals, at the first opportunity, that he is incapable of making a decision (Benjamin 2003, p.71).

We should consider carefully what this incapacity to decide could actually mean. It should be clear that the way to take this argument seriously must not be to argue that the sovereign is incapable of deciding with regard to the realm of law. The baroque sovereign was certainly capable of deciding in that realm—he and later sovereigns are all capable of suspending the rule of law in favour of some exceptional regime. Instead, the sovereign's incapacity to decide pertains to the realm in which Schmitt's debate with Benjamin takes place, namely the state of exception itself. But this puts the sovereign in a curious position. This is so because the sovereign decision on the exception—as Schmitt talks about it—is a decision taken in a normal situation. In the normal situation the sovereign can decide on the exception. The sovereign is capable of deciding that an exception should be made to the rule, but once the rule is suspended, the sovereign is not really capable of deciding anything else. He can use all his might to strike down upon dissidents, terrorists, demonstrators and others who might annoy him, but he can make no further decisions because there is nothing more to suspend. He cannot decide on the suspension of that which has already been suspended. In this way there is a certain kind of helplessness to the figure of the sovereign. His ultimate power is in a way also his weakness. The power of Schmitt's sovereign is one-directional, and that in the end makes it very difficult for him to exert the power Schmitt wants him to exert, if we read *Political Theology* as a response to Benjamin's *Critique of Violence* in the way Agamben does. Deciding on the exception is much easier in the normal situation than it is when the exception is already in place.

The ultimate argument in Agamben's rehearsal of the debate between Benjamin and Schmitt is the famous eighth thesis from *Theses on the Philosophy of History* (Benjamin 1968), in which he states: 'The history of the oppressed teaches us that the state of exception in which we live is the rule' (Benjamin 1968 VII). The point of the argument is that we can no longer really say that there is a situation of normalcy anywhere. The political and juridical system is in a state of permanent crisis, of permanent more or less explicit suspension.

This notion is truly devastating for Schmitt's sovereign. Agamben spells out the problem as follows: 'From Schmitt's perspective, the functioning of the juridical order ultimately rests on an apparatus—the state of exception—whose purpose is to make the norm applicable by temporarily suspending its efficacy. When the exception becomes the rule, the machine can no longer function' (Agamben 2005a, p.58). Here again Agamben points out that Schmitt's ultimate idea with the much-maligned notion of theological sovereignty is to keep the norm in place. The norm can only be kept in place if there is a mechanism that can suspend it from time to time, but this mechanism only works as long as we can tell the emergency situation from the normal situation and the normal legal paradigm from the exceptional one. Sovereign power is the power to switch between clearly defined legal situations of normalcy and exception. But the moment there is no way of telling the one from the other, that is the moment where the sovereign's incapacity to decide sets in. Here, there can be no concentration of power, because each and every time the attempt is made to suspend the legal normality, the result can only be a further blurring of the lines that separate normalcy and exception. What we get in this situation is not a centralized power that gathers all capacities in the hands of very few, but rather a glaring lack of the possibility to know where power is and what it can do. It is precisely this situation which is a situation of iustitium rather than one of dictatorship.

This is the warning Agamben present us with: the more exceptional legal rules are introduced into the normal rule of law, the more we become incapable of knowing what is the norm and what is the rule, the more will we find ourselves *not* in a situation where certain individuals and institutions have too much power and too many capacities, but instead in a situation where the law simply cannot be known, a situation in which legal systems as such become more and more like a tragic drama than anything remotely assembling institutions of justice.

Auctoritas and Potestas

In the state of exception, understood as iustitium rather than dictatorship, law and exception blur and become a zone of indistinction. Another way to put this point is that the situation takes on a *life of its own*. Law stops being a rule to be followed, and exception stops being clearly defined outside of the rule. Both become un-interpretable and in-distinguishable. And this un-interpretability is what we should understand as *life* in this regard. Agamben accentuates this by pointing to a letter from Benjamin to Gershom Scholem, in which he writes 'the Scripture without its key is not Scripture, but life' (Agamben 2005a, p.63). This notion of life, of law and exception together as life, is the notion of a force. It a force Agamben has taken great care to define in chapter 3 of the book as force-of-~~law~~. This neologism deserves an introduction.

In the state of normality, the law can be said to have a certain force. By law we can put people in jail, we can redistribute wealth, we can even go to war. We may understand force-of-law as this capacity of the law to do things. But it is not only the law in the strict sense that has this power. In parliamentary democracies it is the representatives of the people in parliament that have the power to form new laws, but as a matter of fact decrees formulated by the executive branch of government can equally well have the force of law, even though they are not laws in the strict sense. Agamben's notion of the force-of-~~law~~ is the notion of this force, but in the situation where it has completely severed its tie to the law—for instance if the legislature has no real control over the decrees issued by the executive. The thing Agamben calls life by quoting the letter from Benjamin to Scholem is this force freed of any constraints. This is what we find in the permanent state of exception. In this situation the force-of-law is still functioning, but it is completely freed from the letters of the law that bind it to specific purposes and guarantees that citizens can know what it will do. When the state of exception becomes the rule the predictability of the law disappears because the conflation of rule and exception severs the link between law and force-of-law—hence the expression force-of-~~law~~.

At this point it is probably fair to ask whether it is in fact true that the state of exception is becoming permanent. Here, we can to a greater extent rely upon the analyses conducted by empirical scholars of the history of jurisprudence. What we need to look for in this regard is not a question of iustitium versus dictatorship, as would have been the case in my discussion above, but rather a question about the exception versus normalcy. Plenty of studies supply us with evidence of the fact that whenever exceptional measures are introduced to deal with emergencies, the general tendency is that they eventually become the norm. Indeed, in terms of anti-terror legislation—which is one very pertinent example—it is very hard to separate exception from norm (see e.g. Gross & Ní Aoláin 2006).

For Agamben this situation means that we need to introduce new theoretical concepts. His strategy is again the archaeological excavation of the conceptual structures that at one point in history were very clear and available to consciousness, but since then have been forgotten without losing their significance—they have in other words become unconscious. Thus, Agamben again takes the road back to Roman law, where he uncovers the conceptual pair *auctoritas* and *potestas*.

Agamben begins by noticing that the power of the Roman Senate is usually termed auctoritas, and that this in many ways can and has been interpreted as a lesser form of power than the more direct potestas. Hannah Arendt, for instance, argues that the power of the senate was that of giving advice (Arendt 1990, p.200). Agamben makes the same thing clear by pointing out the following: 'The Senate cannot express itself without being questioned by the magistrates and can only request or "counsel"—*consultum* is the technical term—without this "counsel" ever being absolutely binding. The formula of the *senatus consultum* is *si eis videatur*, "if it seems right to them [i.e., the magistrates]"' (Agamben 2005a, p.77). However, what Agamben asks us to consider is that the Senate's auctoritas was also responsible for announcing iustitium. Iustitium was announced as the ultimate authority of the senate: the *senatus consultum ultimum*. 'What previous attempts to understand this relation [of potestas and auctoritas] have not taken into account is precisely that extreme figure of *auctoritas* that is at issue in the *senatus consultum ultimum* and the *iustitium*' (Agamben 2005a, p.78). In this extreme case, the auctoritas of the senate would seem to be something quite different from merely giving advice, because with the senatus consultum ultimum the state of iustitium would immediately be in force, but this does not mean that the senate suddenly could be said to have possessed potestas, which would the more straightforward legal power or right. In the Roman Republic potestas originated with the Roman people and was delegated to the magistrates. The Senate in the Republic could never, for instance, never have issued an order, which would have been a clear case of potestas.

In order to understand the notion of auctoritas entailed in the senatus consultum ultimum, Agamben refers to Roman private law, where auctoritas was a commonly used concept. Here, auctoritas is that which confers legal validity upon an action that would otherwise not have had it. For instance, in marital law 'the *auctoritas* of the father "authorizes"— that is, makes valid—the marriage of the son *in potestate*' (Agamben 2005a, p.76). In this way, auctoritas should be understood as that which enacts. It is not the power to say how things should be, but rather that which makes real the things that have already been said should be real (the son is capable of choosing for himself that he should marry, but it is the auctoritas of the father that authorizes his choice).

A comparison with an order will again be useful. Orders are injunctions that can be followed or rejected. They set up rules but, crucially, they have to be enforced in order to make a difference. An order without force can easily be ignored. This force, on the other hand, is precisely auctoritas. Agamben points out that linguistic studies of the Roman language confirm this point. Following Emilie Benveniste, auctoritas originates in the verb *augeo*, which means to perfect or to augment.

In the normal situation the relation between potestas and auctoritas is one where potestas means an established prerogative or power and auctoritas means the enactment of that power. This fits nicely with the example from marital law above, but also with what we would expect from the relation between an order and its enactment. Normally, we assume that an order needs to be given before it can be enacted. Thus, potestas normally precedes auctoritas.

However, relying again upon the linguistic work of Benveniste, Agamben argues that auctoritas 'denotes not the increase of something which already exists, but the act of producing from one's own breast; a creative act' (Agamben 2005a, p.76). The point is that the relation between auctoritas and potestas can also be the obverse of the normal situation; auctoritas does not need potestas to be predefined in order to be able to act. The life of the force-of-~~law~~ is an auctoritas uncontrolled by potestas. It is this living 'law' that Agamben thinks we should accustom ourselves to thinking about when we are debating current issues of politics, law and exception. Far too often these debates take place in terms of potestas, meaning in the terms of who has the prerogative or capacity to decide and act in certain extreme circumstances; but the Agambendian point is that the acts that are undertaken in the state of exception do not correspond to such clearly defined powers. Rather, it is a strange notion that is much more difficult to grasp and, hence, to criticize that we should be worried about: the living law that is the authority of the law without the law.

What enters the scene in this situation where law and life coincide is bio-politics. It is bio-politics, not only in the sense we saw in connection with Agamben's analysis in *Homo Sacer* where the production of pure life as an *object* of sovereign power was concluded to be crucial for the functioning of sovereignty. Instead, it is bio-politics in the sense that the *subject* of sovereign power itself is understood as life. What is more, this particular kind of power as life, as authority, is something Agamben identifies as a common theme of the great political catastrophes in the 20th centuries. Especially in fascism, we find that the figure of the *duce* or the *führer* is not simply a person of power who rules the nation in despotic fashion, but rather is a body incorporating the force of the law without the law dictating what can and cannot be done in advance.

According to Agamben, this is what we should be worried about when we are considering the contemporary juridico-political situation. In the situation where the exception becomes the norm, we are not only confronted with more or less secret state organizations such, as such as a security police and intelligence agencies, but rather a situation where the capacities and prerogatives of the agents of the state are fundamentally unknowable. The problem is not only that certain institutions have prescribed capacities to act in ways that could be unjust. It is rather that they embody the authority to simply act without restraint. In this situation, the meaning of the law begins to disappear. If auctoritas becomes to clearly detached from potestas, i.e., if the exception is becoming permanent, then auctoritas simply becomes its own potestas. This is a strange but, nonetheless, crucial logic. The clear separation of auctoritas from potestas, i.e. the purification of auctoritas, means that it becomes *identical* with potestas. In this situation, the very enactment of the absence of a law automatically becomes law. The brute force in simply acting becomes its own legitimization in the situation where no other form of legitimacy can be found.

This point brings us back to the ontological considerations from which we set out. What we encounter here is once again the indifference between pure actuality and pure potentiality I elaborated above. To see why, it suffices to consider the point that we should understand potestas as the legal notion of a potentiality. To have potestas is to be given a power in the sense of a possibility of acting in a certain way. But in order to enact that power, something other than potestas is needed, namely auctoritas, which we should understand as the legal term for actualization. In ontological terms, Agamben's analysis of the state of exception therefore stands as the validation of the ontological point that the purification of potentiality and actualization (i.e. their complete separation from each other), has as its logical consequence that they become identical. In this identity, and in the peculiar but nevertheless completely concrete and observable political and juridical situations where it is played out, we find the full extent of Agamben's notion of a zone of indistinction.

Agamben ends his analysis in *State of Exception* with a notion of pure activity in the sense of auctoritas. This analysis should give us some very much needed conceptual tools with which we can begin to interpret and understand what happens when emergencies (be they real or merely perceived) take place and exceptional measures are taken. What we encounter in these situations is more than anything else a call to immediate action. In general, what is actually being done is much less of a concern, and in the final analysis the consequences of the actions taken tend to be more or less irrelevant. 'Do something!' is often the fundamental call. This is a call for auctoritas. It is a call for power to transform itself into pure activity. To convince oneself of the validity of this (perhaps disheartening) analysis, one merely needs to think of the things that usually happen whenever terrorist attacks take place. There will immediately be a crucial and frantic activity in all relevant parts of government. The only thing in such a situation that is completely unthinkable is that governments would remain inactive.

In this way we can see how Agamben's archaeological investigation of the concepts of auctoritas and potestas can help us understand what we unconsciously tend to do in emergency situations, even though we consciously debate these situations very differently. Unconsciously, we often act in terms of auctoritas, but all our debates tend to concentrate on notions of potestas. We consciously think of the state of exception in terms of dictatorship, but the reality of it is often one that resembles iustitium.

Chapter 4: Economic Theology. On *The Kingdom and the Glory*

The Kingdom and the Glory carries the subtitle *Homo Sacer II,2*. This should catch our immediate attention, as *State of Exception* has the subtitle *Homo Sacer II,1*. *The Kingdom and the Glory* is in other words conceived as the second part of the argument put forward in the book I have discussed in the previous chapter. They should be seen as two sides to the same coin. To see what this means it can be helpful to notice that Agamben brings the notions of potestas and auctoritas with him in *The Kingdom and the Glory*. Thus we read the following in the Preface:

> The double structure of the governmental machine, which in *State of Exception* appeared in the correlation between *auctoritas* and *potestas*, here takes the form of the articulation between Kingdom and Government and, ultimately, interrogates the very relation—which initially was not considered—between oikonomia and glory, between power as governmental and effective management, and power as ceremonial and liturgical reality (Agamben 2011, pp.xi–xii).

The difference Agamben spells out here, between *State of Exception* and *The Kingdom and the Glory*, is that the former ended with a point about the pure *activity* of power (auctoritas), whereas the latter ends with a crucial idea of the *inactivity* of power—an inactivity he identifies as glory.

Before we can reach the point Agamben makes about glory towards the end of the book, we first have to acquaint ourselves with the analyses he presents throughout the first five chapters of the book. Here, he deals with a notion that must come as a surprise for modern ears: economic theology. Where *State of Exception* is conceived within the Schmittian paradigm of political theology (even though it takes us, as we have seen, quite far away from Schmitt and closer to Benjamin) *The Kingdom and the Glory* takes as its point of departure the work of Erik Peterson, a catholic theologian who had a significant dispute with Schmitt on the concept of political theology.. Agamben does not take sides in the debate; instead, he is interested in the omissions that become apparent when one takes a closer look.

First, even though Peterson argues that a political theology (i.e. Schmitt's invention and the background of his theory of sovereignty) is strictly speaking impossible, they still share a fundamental idea: namely katechon. We have already touched upon Schmitt's understanding of katechon above. Katechon is the theological concept of a restrainer; it is that which prevents the arrival of the end of time. The main difference between Schmitt and Peterson is that where Schmitt interprets katechon as a political concept, Peterson sees it as strictly a concept of culture—hence his argument that political theology is impossible.

Second, there is a crucial omission in their debate on the viability of political theology that reaches all the way back to a consideration of the earliest Christian theology in the Church Fathers. Neither Schmitt nor Peterson pay much attention to the notion of theological *economy*, even though it was a key concept for the Church Fathers' understanding of monotheism (i.e. the monarchy of God that stands in the background of Schmitt's theological idea of sovereignty). Agamben writes:

> An overview of the authors quoted above by Peterson [the Church fathers] in his genealogy of the theological-political paradigm of the divine monarchy shows that, from both a textual and a conceptual point of view, the 'discourse of economy' is so strictly intertwined with that of monarchy that the fact that it is absent in Peterson lets us infer something like a conscious omission (Agamben 2011, p.14).

Agamben calls Peterson's work a genealogy here, but the passage clearly tells us that he thinks a second genealogy that focuses specifically on the notion of economy is needed. This is the task he undertakes in *The Kingdom and the Glory*. Two questions thus confront us: what is entailed in speaking about economy in a theological context, and how does this influence of economy on theology in turn tell us something about the modern political world?

This gives us a clear indication of Agamben's ambition in *The Kingdom and the Glory*. It is an investigation of early and Medieval Christian theology that takes its point of departure in the idea that this theology can be understood as the conceptual genealogy of later modern formations of state and politics. The meticulous descriptions of the divine order, of the relation between God as Father and God as Son, of the hierarchy and relations between angels and of the notion of providence, should all be read as treatises on the organization of power.

It may sound strange that these abstract scholastic theological exercises should be understood in such a secular way, but nonetheless this is the argument put forward by Agamben. Indeed, for him, the investigation of this kind of surprising historical link is an essential part of genealogical studies:

> When we undertake an archaeological research it is necessary to take into account that the genealogy of a political concept or institution may be found in a field that is different from the one in which we initially assumed we would (for instance, it may be found in theology and not in political science) (Agamben 2011, p.112).

Agamben argues for this by saying that 'archaeology is a science of signatures' (ibid.), which he understands as 'something that, in a sign or a concept, exceeds it to refer it back to a specific interpretation or move it to another context, yet without exiting the field of the semiotic to construct a new meaning' (Agamben 2011, p.87). A signature is in other words the very transitory element that enables a concept to move from one particular sphere (i.e. theology) into another one (i.e. politics) without changing its meaning in any fundamental way. Agamben argues that *ordo*, order, is such a signature by virtue of which oikonomia, economy, moves from the field of the household in ancient Greece, to the field of divinity in Christian theology and further on to politics in the modern times. The crucial point now is, for Agamben, that the fact that oikonomia moved in this way tells us something essential about the political, cultural and historical development of the West.

Agamben is quite clear about the analytical force he attributes to this insight:

> Bringing these questions back to their theological dimension—questions that seem to find only trivial answers on the level of political and social logical investigations—has allowed us to catch a glimpse of something like the ultimate structure of the governmental machine of the West in the relation between *oikonomia* and glory. The analysis of doxologies and liturgical acclamations, of ministries and angelic call him is turned out to be more useful for the understanding of the structures and functioning of power than many pseudo-philosophical analyses of popular sovereignty, the rule of law, or the communicative procedures that regulate the formation of public opinion and political will (Agamben 2011, p.xii).

The Genealogy of Oikonomia

In *The Kingdom and the Glory*, Agamben takes one more step away from the Schmittian point about sovereignty we saw him introduce in *Homo Sacer* above. Instead of political theology, he argues that the central modality of power in the occident today is (theological) economy. It should be noted straight away that this is not identical to a simplified idea that money rules the world. The question here is not 'Who has the most power?' but rather (and much more important) 'How does power function?' That the crucial form of power today is economy does not simply mean that those with more money have more power. It means that the functioning of power is that of 'administration of the household', which is Agamben's translation of the Ancient Greek term oikonomia (Agamben 2011, p.17).

This translation, which brings Agamben back to Aristotle (ibid.), is important because, as Agamben points out, there has been a long tradition for understanding the Church Fathers' use of oikonomia as 'divine plan of salvation.' The crucial point here thus relates directly back to the methodological point of the investigation of signatures made above. What Agamben is arguing is that when the Church Fathers made use of oikonomia, they indeed meant what they were saying. They did not take up the word in order to completely transform its meaning and turn it into a specific theological concept of salvation. He spends quite some time making this argument, going over important passages from Paul, Justin, Theophilus of Antioch and Irenaeus, and shows that whenever these authors write oikonomia they mean precisely the same as Aristotle did when he used the concept to describe the administration of a house (oikos). When the Church Fathers speak of divine oikonomia, they simply mean the divine household. They use the term to try to make sense of how God has organized his estate in the then very recent religious invention: Christianity.

Agamben makes a convincing argument for this point by showing that the Church fathers introduced oikonomia into theology with a specific purpose, namely to answer the question of the relation between monotheism and trinity: How can God be one, if he is also three? For the Church fathers this was a crucial problem, because the doctrine of trinity comes with inherent danger of a fall back into polytheism.[1]

The idea of divine oikonomia became the solution for the Church Fathers to these questions. According to Agamben, they argued that, just as the power of the patron of a household (oikos) would remain undivided and his own (even though he could bestow administrative duties onto his son or some other worthy person), so too could the being of God remain one, even though he would let his Son administer the divine household and run the divine economy (in other words, do the job of saving the souls of men). In early Christianity, Agamben thus finds that what the apostle Paul calls 'economy of the mystery' is an absolutely central idea (Agamben 2011, p.23). It is this formu-

---

1   Agamben's only focus in this regard is the relation between Father and Son. He brackets the question of the third part of Trinity, the Holy Spirit, because, as he argues, it did not become a crucial problem until the fourth century, and the crucial developments he is tracking had already taken place in the first and second centuries (Agamben 2011, p.44).

lation of an economy of the mystery that, according to Agamben, has given rise to the misnomer that economy in Christianity should signify the divine plan of salvation. While economy has to do with salvation, when the word is being used in a theological context, the meaning of it remains the same as it ever was—it simply means management of the household.

This point is important for Agamben because, if one ignores it, it becomes very difficult to grasp what happened when the Pauline formula 'economy of the mystery' was inverted by the Church Father Hyppolytus into 'mystery of the economy':

> While, in Paul, the economy was an activity carried out to reveal or accomplish the mystery of God's will or word (Colossians 1:24-25; Ephesians 3:9),[1] now it is this very activity, personified in the figure of the son-word, that becomes a mystery (Agamben 2011, p.38).

The solution to the problem of squaring monotheism with the divinity of both Father and Son entailed a distinction between God's being and God's activity in the form of oikonomia. Thus, this activity itself became a mystery. In this way, the original solution to the problem of monotheism in Christianity itself became a new problem. After Hyppolytus, it was no longer the splitting of the divine figure into two persons that was the issue—it was rather the split between being and action.

The split between being and action placed the Church fathers at a crossroads. If being and action are split, what could then be said of the being of action? If Christ's being is founded in the being of the Father, then there is no separation of being and action, and thus there is no solution to the problem of the relation between the unity and the trinity of God. On the other hand, if the Son were not founded in the being of the Father, then it would seem to deepen the issues of upholding monotheism. The Church Fathers chose the second route. They gathered around the idea that the being of Christ is anarchi-

---

1   Agamben pays no attention to the fact that several of Paul's letters, including Colossians and Ephesians, today have been determined by biblical exegetic scholarship to not have been written by Paul.

cal, meaning without foundation. Christ was eventually argued to be every bit as autonomous and original as God himself. In this way the ontological God, the God-as-One, eventually became superfluous. What remained was the pure anarchical action of God-as-Son. The cover of *The Kingdom and the Glory* shows an image that describes this development quite nicely. It depicts an empty throne. This empty throne of God (it can be seen in many Paleochristian and Byzantine basilicas (Agamben 2011, p.xiii)) was the result of the theological developments that originated in the discussion of the divine economy by the Church Fathers. This image shows the solution to the problem of monotheism entailed in the split between being and action. Action came to be the dominant concept, and being slowly turned into an afterthought.

That this is not simply an arcane problem of ancient theology is made evident by Agamben as he points out that this is really the historical moment of the separation of being and language. In Ancient Greek philosophy, logos had a secure foundation in ousia and cosmos—indeed, the ousia (being) of cosmos was simply identical to logos (language). In the philosophical/theological tradition that followed after the theology of Church Fathers, like Hyppolytus, the very relation between language (or thought) and being would become the fundamental problem. To see the crucial difference between the ancient world and the world that would begin to emerge with Christianity, all one needs to do is to compare the distinction between being and action that follows from the economic model of divinity in Christianity with the being and action of Aristotle's unmoved mover. The Aristotelian God moved the celestial spheres, not because of a special will or care for the world, but out of the pure necessity of his own nature. This identity between being and praxis in God was severed by the introduction of the concept of oikonomia into Christian theology.

If we take this doctrine and read it as Agamben does (i.e. as a genealogical origin of the present day system of politics), the anarchy of Christ means that political action is itself set free. Political guidelines can no longer be derived from the idea of God. In this sense Christ takes us beyond political theology. However, following Agamben,

this does not result in political emancipation. It does not even provide the conceptual structure for a subsequent political emancipation. The story of theological economy is not a story of the prefigura-
tion of modern liberalism in Christianity. Rather, it is the other way
around. That which is understood as modern liberalism, should in
truth be seen as simply a formation of power, which is reminiscent of
the formations of power developed in early Christianity. The crucial
point is that, with the liberation of politics from Being-as-One, man
does not simply receive the responsibility for dealing with his own
future. The liberation of politics from God-as-One merely means that
the administrative duties are passed along to God-as-Son. Politics
moves from theological ontology to theological economy. It is not
the sovereign—and certainly not the sovereign people—but rather
the minister and the administrator who are in power. Or to be precise:
the centre of power has been emptied, but the minister is still keeping house with persons and things from his position right next to the
empty centre.

What is revealed by Agamben in this first part of the genealogical
investigation in *The Kingdom and the Glory* is thus the emergence of
the administrative paradigm of politics. This notion of politics not as
sovereign action from a central point of power, but rather as vicarious
administration from a peripheral point, has already emerged in early
Christian theology and not as a result of enlightenment processes.
His argument is thus directly linked to the debate on secularization
that took place in the 1960s in Germany. Here, philosophers such as
Hans Blumenberg, Karl Löwith, Odo Marquand and (of course) Carl
Schmitt eagerly debated the legitimacy of the notions of secularization and modernity. The key thesis—the ignition of the debate—
was Löwith's contention that modern philosophy of history and the
enlightenment's idea of progress are simply secularized versions of
Christian eschatology, where secularization means a transfer of a
religious idea into a secular sphere, and thus the very opposite of a
liberation from the religious forms of power that the term is often
taken to mean in everyday use. Agamben agrees with the critique of
secularization, even though he argues that Löwith and others make
the argument from weak premises, because they have not conducted

the thorough archaeological investigation he himself has. Crucially, this means that all of the participants in the German debate discuss the notions of the philosophy of history and the enlightenment from false premises. In fact, he points out, one of the more scorned philosophers of history, Friedrich Wilhelm Joseph Schelling, was much closer to the truth than any of his modern critics, precisely because he discussed the notion of theological economy in his philosophy of revelation (Agamben 2011, p.5).

The first part of Agamben's book ends with the conclusion that the modern religion par excellence is bureaucracy. The analysis follows the trajectory laid out by *State of Exception* in the way that it seeks to help us focus differently when we are discussing and investigating politics today. All too often, when we are debating the political events that shape our lives, we tend to focus exclusively on the person or the seat of power we believe is responsible for our plight. Our critique often ends with the point that somebody must take the fall when things go wrong. But more often than not the seat of power we rebel against was empty from the start. The empty chair as the seat of power is a precise metaphor for the administrative regime because it is not the King but rather his plethora of ministers and advisors that should be our focus. Theologically speaking, we should be more concerned with God's angels than with God himself.

If democracy can at times seem a futile project, it is because what representative democracy has accomplished—if taken to the core—has been to exchange a King for the people. We exchanged the sovereign monarch with the sovereign people. But the seat is still empty and the power is still administered from the offices of ministers. *State of Exception* calls our attention not to the decisions made by persons identified with power—as in the dictatorship model—but rather to the much less uniform state of emergency as it is understood in the iustitium model. *The Kingdom and the Glory* calls our attention to a similar point by investigating the paradigm of governmental thought in Christian theology, from which Agamben argues that we have adopted it in modern democracies.

Angels and their offices

As the doctrine of divine economy evolved and became an elaborate theory of providence, it was also extended to include angelology. One could say that it was no longer enough for the Father of the divine house to have his son manage it; it became necessary to include a range of angels as well. This means that we can read the scholastic doctrines on the numbers and types of angels in a completely different light than usually is the case. At least if we follow Agamben, we can read the arcane discussions on angels in scholasticism as elaborate theories of the organization of power. The figure of the angel can even be said to be the most central point of emphasis in *The Kingdom and the Glory*. That is so because the angel is the figure that brings together the two terms 'kingdom' and 'glory'

Where the first part of the book deals with the notion of divine activity (in the sense of oikonomia) the second part of the book deals with the notion of glory as it is produced by ceremonies, liturgies and acclamations. The figure of the angel is the link between these two parts of Agamben's analysis, because the angel in scholastic theology served to accomplish these two precise tasks: on the one hand, the angels had to do the administrative work of providence (they were, in other words, the extended arm of the office introduced into Christianity with the figure of Christ); and on the other hand the angels had the task of singing hymns to the glory of God.

For Agamben, this provides an opportunity for asking and answering a question which—to his mind—is curiously underplayed in political theory and philosophy: Why does Power need glory? (Agamben 2011, p.12). The usual answer given to this question is often accepted as a matter of course: power needs glory for instrumental reasons. The idea is that power needs glory because through glory people can be brought to accept the exertion of power; power needs glory in the same way as it needs entertainment and—in general—what in a Marxist tradition can be summarized as ideology. What Agamben could be said to do with his genealogy of glory is thus to correct the assumption of instrumentalism that pervades many contemporary critiques of ideology. This investigation has the aim of showing us an alternative that makes it clear that the relation of power and glory is even more intimate than can be conceived under the heading of 'instrumentalism'.

Agamben argues that the problem with instrumentalism is that it entails an external relation between power and glory. If glory is understood as a means to uphold power, then it inevitably must be understood as something other than power, something that is not itself power but which nevertheless enables power to function. To take a pertinent example: for the Roman Emperor, triumphs and parades were important ways of achieving glory. Here, the instrumentalist analysis would say that while this glory may have helped the Emperor stay in power, in itself triumph and parades were something quite different from his actual power to rule the realm. Following Agamben, this is wrong. In the transition from the Republic to the Empire, the triumph played a much more direct role, simply because it was the only time at which magistrates had the right to bear arms and to have their followers bear them in the city (Agamben 2011, p.183).

Another pertinent example is found in the fasces:

> The fasces were elm or birch rods about 130 centimeters in length, bound together with a red strap into which an axe was inserted laterally. They were assigned to a special corporation, half *apparitores* and half executioners, called *lictores*, who wore the fasces on their left shoulder. In the republic, the period about which we have most information, the fasces were the prerogative of the consul and the magistrate who had *imperium*. The lictors, twelve in number, had to accompany the rnagistrate on every occasion, not just on public occasions. When the consul was at home, the lictors waited in the vestibule; if he went out, even if only to the spa or the theater, they invariably accompanied him. (Agamben 2011, p.182)

It is clear that the fasces and the lictores that carried them were primarily ceremonial. Furthermore, since the time of the Republic the fasces has become one of the most powerful and widespread signs of political power in the west. Thus, fascism derives its name from this symbol, and we even find it in US congress. But even though the history of the fasces as a symbol would be one of ceremony and glory, in its original use in Rome it also had a very direct function in terms of power. Agamben even refuses to call them symbols:

> So little does the word symbol characterize them that they in fact served to actually inflict capital punishment in its two forms: flogging (the rods) and decapitation (the axe). (Agamben 2011, p.182).

Agamben's point here is that the fasces present a very nice example of how power and glory can be much more intertwined than the instrumentalist understanding allows for—glory is very often identical to power and power is very often identical to glory. We can expand on this point by taking a look at Agamben's discussion of the choreographed nature of acclamations. One should not take lightly the meticulous way in which acclamations and ceremonies are organized. Agamben goes into depth with an extreme case of the Byzantine Empire. He analyses a treatise on imperial ceremony by Constantine VII Porphyrogenous and shows that 'there is not a gesture, garment, ornament, word, silence, or place that is not ritually fixed or meticulously catalogued' (Agamben 2011, p.184). The point is that acclamations are not simply organized; they are excessively organized. As a mere means to achieve the end of continuation of power the meticulousness of, the regulations of acclamations are excessive.

The key term Agamben points to in explaining this excessive organization of glory is hierarchy. Again, the Byzantine court was exemplary: 'An infinite hierarchy of functionaries and other people [...] watches over the protocol to ensure that it is observed at every moment' (Agamben 2011, p.184). The point Agamben makes is that hierarchy and glory are closely related. Furthermore, he points out that hierarchy and angelology, in particular, are more intimately con-nected than one would normally think:

> The introduction of the theme of hierarchy into angelology—and even the invention of the very term 'hierarchy'—is the work of an apocryphal author whose gesture is one of the most tenacious

mystifications in the history of Christian literature, and it is still waiting to be uncovered (Agamben 2011, p.152).

Agamben argues that the confusion about the origin of the work has led to the unfortunate consequence that the subsequent understanding of the notion of hierarchy has become confused. However, a simple rereading of the text can, as Agamben shows, help us regain clarity about the strategy involved in the introduction of hierarchy:

> It is a case, on the one hand, of placing angels in a hierarchy, arranging their ranks according to a rigidly bureaucratic order and, on the other hand, of angelifying the ecclesiastical hierarchies, by distributing them according to an essentially sacred gradation (Agamben 2011, p.152).

The link between hierarchy and angels has the double function of organising angels in a bureaucratic order and of bestowing divine glory on earthly hierarchies. In this way, glory is from the start intimately linked with power—it *is* power and not just an external instrument for gaining or preserving power. 'As Aquinas rightly notes, [hierarchy] does not mean "sacred order" but "sacred power"' (Agamben 2011, p.153). The ultimate frame of reference of this divine hierarchy is the divine economy that founds the Trinitarian understanding of Christianity. The angelic hierarchies became a theological necessity because of the separation between God's being and God's action. The moment God-as-being no longer stood as the guarantee for divine activity (economic providence), at that moment some other way of controlling this activity was needed. Hierarchy was the principle of organization that was introduced instead. Hierarchy became much more important as the throne of God was emptied. This is an interesting point, because what Agamben discovers here is a certain kind of spontaneity in hierarchical organization; hierarchies do not merely form as a result of enforcement from a point above. They are often something we invent the moment the ultimate reference point of power disappears.

Agamben's genealogical investigations tell us something crucial here. No-one is capable of standing at the very top of a hierarchy.

A hierarchy does not make sense through reference to one ultimate enforcer at the top that subjects everyone else to his bidding; a hierarchy often works best if there is no one at the top. They are established with reference to an endpoint that is never encountered. This tells us something about the problematic idea of a transition from a pre-modern, non-democratic politics of submission and dominance to so-called 'modern democratic' ones. It is not at all certain that the removal of the top of the pyramid of power is going to set us all free. True democracy is not necessarily won by cutting off the top hierarchy of power, because that will often bring about something quite different. It can very easily bring about a much more refined and much more rigid system of dominance.

Summarizing the discussion of angels, we can say that they serve the dual task of administering the divine economy of providence and of dispensing glory. This duality is captured quite nicely in the words of Gregory the Great: angels are divided into *administrators* and *assistants*. The administrators are those who are actively engaged in the work of providence; the assistants are those who do nothing but sing the praise of God. Crucially, it is through the songs of praise that the divine hierarchies are established: 'The hierarchy is a hymnology' (Agamben 2011, p.156). As an establishment of hierarchies, the meticulous regulations involved in ceremonies, liturgies and acclamations begin to make sense. The regulations that describe how, by whom and to whom glory is dispensed are crucial, because through them angels, ministers and—in the end—human being are ordered in very strict hierarchical structures. In this way Agamben is able to argue that the foundation of modern bureaucracy (democratic or otherwise) is found in angelology: 'What is decisive, however, is that long before the terminology of civil administration and government was developed and fixed, it was already firmly constituted in angelology' (Agamben 2011, p.158). In this way we can also begin to see how glory does not simply function as a means to an external end of power, but rather—and crucially—it is an essential part of the very functioning of power itself.

Glory, inactivity, capture

We have seen how Agamben argues that there is an intimate relation between power and glory that goes beyond the mere instrumentalist relation of glory serving as a means to the end of keeping power. As of yet, however, we have not described the most crucial part of Agamben's discussion of angelology. This part is found in the notion of inactivity. It can be brought out by considering the role of angels in eschatology.

In question number 108 Thomas Aquinas poses the following problem: what will become of the manifold of angels after the Last Judgement? (Aquinas 1947 Q108, A7). This is not a simple problem. As we should know by now, even the most arcane conceptions of angelology can have significance for our understanding of the organization of political power. To approach the problem we should recall the two distinct functions served by angels, as described above. The angels are divided in administrators, who are actively engaged in divine governance, and the assistants, who sing the praise of God. After the end of time the need for the first of these tasks disappears, but for Thomas Aquinas, and like-minded thinkers, it is crucial that the dispensing of glory continues. Thus, after the Last Judgement the angels continue to sing the praise of God and hence prolong the hierarchical structure of the organization of life for all eternity. This indicates that the dispersal of glory is of an entirely different sort than the actual acts of governance, even though the two are intimately connected, as we have seen.

This may seem like a dilemma, but in truth the apparent conflict merely brings out the crucial feature of the relation between power and glory; they relate to each other as activity to inactivity. Glory is essentially something power does, when it is inactive—glory is what power does when it is not actively executing power. It is power captured in inactivity. And what is perhaps even more important: glory is inactivity captured in power. This last formulation of capturing inactivity in power may sound strange, but it is important for our understanding of Agamben. It relates, in the end, to his specific notion of messianic emancipation, which I will be discussing in the final chapter below. For now, the link between power, glory and inactivity adds further substance to Agamben's argument for why the instrumentalist explanation of glory is wrong.

Instrumentalism thinks of glory as a means to an end. This means that it must think of glory as a certain kind of activity (one could call it an activity of glorifying power). Glory is thought of as something one *does*. It is something that is actively made, exhibited or worked. In the instrumental light, glory is something, done by someone, in order for something else to happen. Thus, it could, for instance, be argued in an instrumentalist vein that a nation is actively glorified in order to make people accept the state apparatus that administers it. But what Agamben's investigation of the function of glory teaches us is that it works in a slightly different way. Glory functions not as the *activity* of pseudo-power outside of power that upholds power, but rather as the very *inactivity* of power itself. Glory is what power does when it does nothing.

We find this inactivity of power very clearly depicted in certain forms of language. It is available to us where language does nothing. Examples of this inactivity are readily available in traditional acclamations, such as the fascist 'Duce, Duce!' or the Nazi 'Sieg Heil!'; we find it in the endless repetitions of 'Holy', 'Sanctus' and 'Amen' in the Christian Church. Here, language stops signifying in any meaningful sense and instead begins to merely repeat patterns of sound. This inactive language, which says nothing and does nothing actively, but which nevertheless succeeds in establishing hierarchies, is the language of glory.

In the language of glory we find power captured in inactivity. It is a notion that brings us back to the ontological point that has been our companion throughout this introduction to the work of Giorgio Agamben. We are confronted, once again, with a zone of indistinction. It is not the case that there is a clear distinction at the bottom of political ontology between the realm of power and that which is outside it. The idea of a fundamental distinction between power and anarchy is wrong. What we encounter when we search the limits of political power is not something antithetical to power, but rather simply power in its mode of inactivity. When we approach the limits of power, we do not find anarchy, we instead enter a zone of indistinction between power and anarchy, where power is not actively engaged in executing power, but where it is present nonetheless in the form of glorious hierarchy.

It is interesting that the language of glorious hierarchy is easy to find in contemporary societies. For instance, we encounter acclamations at football stadiums, where they can take very strictly regulated forms. It might be argued that what happens at football stadiums has nothing to do with politics—that it is merely a recreational activity. That, however, would not contradict what Agamben is saying. The world of sports today serves as a very nice example of glory. Here, political power is very much inactive, and the outcome is a world that is thoroughly hierarchical. Everything in sports is about hierarchies. There is, of course, winning and losing, but there are also the endless rankings of best players, best managers, best fans, best stadiums and best hot dogs. The crucial point about hierarchies in sports is that they are without ultimate purpose. There is no ultimate reason for these hierarchies; there are no final winners. Just as in theological economy the throne of sports is necessarily empty, even if your team wins the championship, there is another one to be won next year, or in four years. In sports, hierarchies have no head, and that is the very reason why they must be enforced and empowered at all cost all the time. In sports, political power is idle, but in this idleness we find an unbroken world of submission and dominance. There is no active power in this world—at least there need not be—but it is still completely hierarchical. This is a perfect image of glory.

The analogy of sports can be extended to the general public sphere without too much difficulty. In public debates we repeatedly encounter references to certain values, concepts or norms that are not genuinely discussed or debated, but simply affirmed or rather glorified. Democracy, human rights and freedom of speech are all popular topics in the public life of Western democracies today, but for all the talk it is crucial to note how little content is in fact being given to these terms. More often than not, they will serve not as topics of actual discussions, but rather as markers for differentiation and the establishment of hierarchies. There are those who are 'affirming strongly' the values of X, and they will be scorning those, who do not 'affirm strongly enough' the values of X. Furthermore, there will be anxious talk about those, who are opposed to the values of X, and about those who are a danger to them. The point is that the most fundamental concepts in the ordering of public life tend to be those that have the least actual content. Slowly but surely those terms are emptied and the use of them is turned into pure acclamations.

The best example of modern political acclamations is found in the context of political economy (in the non-theological sense). Political discussions on economy have their very own acclamation today: it is called 'necessity'. In this concept we can find the work of the modern angels in full visibility. On the one hand, we have the administrators (i.e. the economic angels) who carefully govern the world by calculating its economic necessities, and on the other hand we have the assistants, who sing the praise of this regime by doing nothing other than calling the economic calculation necessary. What has effectively disappeared from this picture is the notion that political economy might be political (i.e. that it might entail something that has the character of a decision). Instead of a political theology we get a theological economy.

In this way, Agamben's genealogical investigation can help us provide a surprising diagnosis of certain contemporary political trends. His studies of angelology also function as a critique of the contemporary administrative regime in the way that they show us just how much modern administration has in common with medieval theology and angelology. Both are systems of glorious hierarchy. It is important to note, however, that Agamben is not nostalgic about politics in the way that Schmitt would have been if he had been presented with the current regime of economic necessity. For Agamben, the return to a more Schmittian model of sovereign decisions would not be much of an improvement over the headless bureaucratic machinery of theological economy. As we saw above, his more Schmittian analyses do not propose Schmitt as a solution. Instead, they utilize Schmitt in order to diagnose the paradoxical problems involved in our notion of sovereignty. Therefore, given the choice between political theology and theological economy, the correct Agambendian answer would be to say that they are both worse. His positive proposal—which we will approach in the final chapter—takes us in a very different direction.

Before we get that far, there is another point about Agamben's analysis of glory that I think it is important to note, as it has some impact on the way we think about the contemporary political situation—especially with regard to the question of law, rights and the state of exception. What Agamben shows us is that there is a place in the universe of power where power is merely inactive and unproductive instead of actually doing something. This is a place that functions very differently than the more obvious uses of power found in declarations of wars, identifications of enemies and announcements of states of exception. In the early years following 9/11, we witnessed a great deal of these kinds of direct acts of power. Wars were started, exceptional legislation was introduced, people were incarcerated, expelled and tortured, etc. After a while, as the immediate obsession with the threat of terror disappeared from the Western mind, so too did the interest for and outrage over the problematic juridical and political situation we were left with as the result of the immediate and very actual reactions of power. It is at this point that the inactivity of power begins to be most relevant. Seen in the light of the political actions taken in the first decade after the attacks on 9/11, one of the most violent things power can do today is to do nothing at all. In other words, to leave the exceptional measures and curtailments of basic rights exactly as they are, after a decade of compromises, is every bit as scandalous as the initial compromises. Indeed, it could in many ways be said to be worse. Today it is the inactivity of power that should interest us rather than its activity, insofar as we wish to criticize the prevailing juridical political regime.

Chapter 5: Messianic profanations

Towards the end of the last chapter on *The Kingdom and the Glory*, I introduced the notion of power captured in inactivity. This is the form of power we encounter in sacred hierarchies. But I also introduced another way of linking the three terms: power, glory and inactivity. I said that glory is inactivity captured in power. Following Agamben, this could easily be said to be the most important link between glory and inactivity. That is the case because this formulation 'glory is inactivity captured in power' only makes sense against the background of Agamben's notion of messianism. This idea takes us back to the ontological discussion of potentiality and freedom I presented in Chapter 1 above. Thus, with this final chapter on messianism, this book comes full circle. In this way I hope it will give a comprehensive understanding of the whole that is Agamben's philosophical endeavour.

In the final chapter of *The Kingdom and the Glory*, Agamben argues that glory is the thing power does when it does nothing—but not only that. Glory is more than the idle production of hierarchy that is achieved by the inactivity of power; glory is also a way of capturing the fundamental inactivity of human life within the structure of power. We have already encountered the fundamental inactivity of life in the examples of Bartleby and Tiananmen above. What remains to be seen is how they relate to Agamben's understanding of the messianic.

We saw how Agamben, in the story of Bartleby, identifies a freedom that is of a different kind than the freedom of choice and yet which is much more fundamental: the freedom of inactivity, the freedom to prefer not to. And we saw how Agamben found this particular form of freedom in the protests on Tiananmen Square, where the relative absence of determinate demands was, for him, not the failure of the protests but rather their most crucial feature. To use a more recent example, we could find the very same element in the initial protests of the Occupy Wall Street movement. They were united under the slogan 'What is our one demand?'

Agamben sees in these kinds of movements neither a form of inde- cisiveness nor a lack of conviction, but rather a refusal to meet the institutions against which they are protesting on the conditions defined by those institutions. The moment such protests become lured into saying definitively what they want, the moment they appoint leaders to negotiate those demands, that is the moment they accept the legiti- macy of the institutions they are protesting against. Thereby, they accept the realm of possibilities those institutions have to offer. In the negotiations that might follow from such acceptance, the move- ments may gain some results and force through some concessions, but they will lose the overall struggle against the very form of politics they are fighting against. Just as we saw Agamben argue in relation to Tiananmen, the true political struggle cannot be over the control of the state. And that is what protesters who end up in negotiations with agents of the state must accept. In any negotiations within the current form of representational politics, one must accept that political power is organized in, and executed by, bureaucratic structures that have the state form of organization. This is a form of organization which, as we have seen, is far from innocent or neutral, and which has a very specific religious genealogy. Agamben's point is that the true politi- cal struggle is the one between the state itself (and its many bureau- cratic forms) and something else, which he calls 'human life'.

It is important to notice that Agamben precisely is not pitting civil society against the state. He is not arguing that there is a community in our public lives where we, as consumers, workers or private per- sons, have a potential struggle against the central bureaucracy of the particular nation states in which we live. These forms of civil society are themselves already structured according to the state form of poli- tics. The two fit each other like hand and glove. In civil society we find private firms, corporations and organizations that in their form and organization are every bit as hierarchical as the central adminis- tration of the nation states.

The essential point of what Agamben calls 'human life' or 'form-of-life' is that it is the antithesis to the hierarchical structure established by these forms of organization. Such an antithesis cannot merely be a negation of those forms, it cannot merely consist in saying 'no' to them, because to do so is already to accept too much. It is already a way of saying 'this rather than that'; it is a way of giving the institutions and organizations something that they may grasp or reject, discuss or negotiate with. This is the reason why Bartleby is such a nice example for Agamben. Bartleby exhibits a kind of resistance that is not a simple protest and which does not merely consist of saying 'no', and which instead takes the shape of inaction. Bartleby leaves only a riddle for the lawyer, a riddle of inactivity. What does Bartleby want? The answer cannot be had because all Bartleby does is to prefer not to. In this way Bartleby can be seen as someone who lives a messianic life.

Having argued this much, we should begin to be able to make sense of the notion of the capture of inactivity in power. Capturing inactivity in power means to take these pockets of messianic inactivity and to reinterpret them in a way that does not leave the state and its organization of power in a state of confusion. It means to take inactivity and to organize it in such a way that it fits with the structure of oikonomia. This is thus the spot where glory serves its most fundamental purpose. Glory has the crucial function of coding every form of human (in)activity in a way that makes it suitable for an economic structure of power. This means that it must first of all serve to make human inactivity hierarchical. It takes something that is inherently unstructured and non-hierarchical—namely inactivity—and makes it something that can be structured according to dominance and submission. The problem for the state and its oikonomia when it encounters figures such as Bartleby is that it finds neither top nor bottom, neither pro nor contra. This means that it cannot do anything with them—it is itself forced into inactivity. The actions of the lawyer in the story of Bartleby, who in the end finds himself leaving the premises of his own office, describe this quite nicely. There is a form of inactivity, a form of human inaction, which cannot be forced.

Bartleby could have been forcibly removed from the premises, just like the protesters in Tiananmen Square were, but if Bartleby in that situation would simply remain inactive, the lawyer would not have gained an inch on him. He would still have been in complete bewilderment. The same can be said about the state with regard to protests like those at Tiananmen.

To be sure, in most of the cases where protests take the shape that Agamben identifies in Tiananmen Square, they eventually amount to very little. In the end, the people participating tire of the ordeal, and go home or back to work. That is the triumph of the state we usually see. But for Agamben, this does not change the fundamental theoretical point; the state does not know what to do with such figures. If it is to act against them, it can only eradicate them in ways that are obviously excessively repressive and brutal. This is the reason why glory is such a crucial feature of state power. What glory does is to capture and make inactivity available in a way that is not dangerous for the state. As long as glory is able to structure inactivity in a hierarchical way, then the state is capable of relating to it without any problems. Glory occupies the space of inactivity in such a way that it does not become problematic for the state and its system of oikonomia.

As if not

Agamben's notion of messianism is paradoxical. This follows from its close connection to his notion of profanation which we have already encountered. In the chapter on *Homo Sacer* above, we saw how Agamben understands religion, not as that which binds together men and gods, but rather as that which creates the original separation between them. Religion consists fundamentally in the gesture that separates the things that are exclusively for the gods and the things that are available for the free use of men. This gives us another and very obvious link between religion and hierarchies. Through the very act of making things separate and certain things exclusive, religion divides not only things but also human beings, and organizes them according their proximity to that which is not to be touched, thereby establishing a religious hierarchy. An important task for the work of glory is thus made clear—it consists of making certain objects exclusive.

As we recall, profanation is the opposite gesture. Paraphrasing Bartleby, we could say that it consists of 'preferring not to' accept the hierarchical injunction. The problem with the idea of profanation is that it seems very difficult to achieve. Indeed, one could rightly ask how it is even possible. If religion is founded on separation, and if hierarchies are established through separations, how does one avoid capture in some glorious religious hierarchy? To not separate, how does one do that? After all, any human action, at least insofar as it is bound up with language, must be concerned with some form of drawing lines and setting up boundaries. As we learned from Saussure and the structuralist tradition, language is primarily a system of differences. A key to understanding how Agamben thinks of profanation in this light is the notion of negligence. Negligence does not eradicate or annul that which it is negligent of. It merely refuses to pay it the proper attention, it refuses 'due respect'. In this way, to be negligent of the separations established by language, law, religion, etc., does not mean to eradicate the boundaries and distinctions that have been set up, but instead to politely ignore them. It means to let the law remain in place, but at the same time to render it inoperative.

Interestingly, Agamben finds the peak of this form of negligence in a genuinely messianic text, one that has since then been captured most effectively by Christianity: Paul's first letter to the Corinthians. Agamben quotes a famous passage:

> But this I say, brethren, the time is short: it remaineth, that both they that have views be as though they had none [*hōs mē*]; and they that weep, as though they wept not; and they that rejoice, as though they rejoiced not; and they that buy, as though they possessed not; and they that use this world, as not abusing it: for the fashion of this world passeth away (1 Corinthians 7:29-31 quoted in Agamben 2011, p.248).

The gesture of negligence, of leaving the law in place while not observing it, is for Agamben captured perfectly in this Pauline text. The Greek *hōs mē* literally means 'as if not'. To profane the law is to accept the law as if one did not accept it. It means to accept that the rules of separation and hierarchy are there, but to behave as if they were not. Agamben has also described this attitude as 'play'—to play with rules means not to obliterate them but rather to use them improperly, without reverence, without accepting the glory they are covered in. Unfortunately, Agamben observes a decline in play:

> Play as an organ of profanation is in decline everywhere. Modern man proves he no longer knows how to play precisely through the vertiginous proliferation of new and old games. Indeed, at parties, in dances, and at play, he desperately and stubbornly seeks exactly the opposite of what he could find there: the possibility of re-entering the lost feast, returning to the sacred and its rites, even in the form of the inane ceremonies of the new spectacular religion or a tango lesson in a provincial dance hall. In this sense, televised game shows are part of a new liturgy; they secularize an unconsciously religious intention. To return to play its purely profane vocation is a political task. (Agamben 2007, pp.76–77)

This is a very acute description of what happens in the glorification of play. When inactivity stops being playful and instead begins to long for the experience of the sacred, that is the moment when the inoperativity of human life becomes captured in the structure and hierarchy of glory. Examples of this tendency abound. In new age spiritualization, in the various ethics of authenticity, in the many common sense moral injunctions 'stay true to yourself', 'be real', 'do your own thing', all of these point towards a new liturgy, or rather towards a reinvention of the old Christian one. Of course, the very best example of this phenomenon is found in the world of sports that we have already touched upon. Here, glory has almost extinguished the notion of play. It is important to note that the criticism of the contemporary regime of organized sports that can be established by drawing upon Agamben's genealogy does not focus on the pecuniary aspect. The problem is not simply that money rules the world of sports, as it rules so many other worlds. The problem is, strictly speaking, glorification. This means that the perceived antidote to the influx of money and power in sports (namely the return to the authentic contest delivered from all cheating, doping, match-fixing, etc.) is every bit as problematic as those 'problems' themselves. Indeed, the entailed notion of authenticity could easily be called the contemporary term for glorification par excellence. The Agambendian antidote to this tendency is the Paulinian or Bartlebyian: to render the ecstatic, the sacred and the authentic inoperative. It is to prefer not to, it is to abide by the rules as if they were not. To play as if one could neither win nor lose.

The End

The beginning of the quote from 1 Corinthians above introduces a notion of temporality which can shed some light on the specific meaning of messianism in Agamben. The messianic is very often read as synonymous with the eschatological. The messianic refers to the coming of the messiah (i.e. to the coming of the end of the present era or, if you will, the end of this world). This would seem to put it on a par with the notion of eschatology, which we have already discussed with reference to Schmitt and Peterson above. Eschatology is the doctrine of the eschaton, i.e. the endpoint of time.

It would seem that messianism and eschatology are entirely alike. Both deal with the coming of the end. Further confusion of the terms follows from the fact that they have been secularized in the modern era in various ways—perhaps most prominently by revolutionary Marxism, where the notion of the revolution very often entailed the idea of the point in time that was to mark the end of one era and the coming of a new one. Indeed, for conservative thinkers like Schmitt and Peterson, the Marxist revolutionary idea of eschatology could easily be identified with the antichrist, and thus a reason for why the notion of katechon plays such an important role in their thinking. As we might recall, the katechon is the restrainer, that which struggles against the coming of the eschaton.

For Agamben, however, it is absolutely essential that we do not conflate the notions of eschatology and messianism. His book on Paul, *The Time that Remains* (Agamben 2005b), makes the most extensive argument for this point. My final reflection in the present book presents Agamben's argument for messianism and against eschatology in *The Time that Remains*. I think ending a book on the notion of the end is a fitting gesture.

Since we have said that both messianism and eschatology deal with notions of time coming to and end, we can introduce a conceptual pair that has a lot of philosophical pedigree: *chronos* and *kairos*. Chronos, and with it chronology, is the concept of time that runs its course. Chronological time is time in its state of normalcy. Kairos, on the other hand, is the notion of time as an instance or a moment; kairos is the point in time that stands out; it is the temporal term for exception. The question of the relation between eschatology and messianism is thus the question of the meaning of kairos. If the only way of interpreting kairos is through the notion of eschaton, then there can be no real differentiation between messianism and eschatology.

Agamben introduces the work of the French linguist Gustave Guillaume in order to present a viable distinction. Guillaume utilized a concept of 'operational time' in his theory of the temporality of verbs, which is all the more interesting for Agamben because it builds on Aristotle's distinction between potentiality and actualization. A central point in Guillaume's theory is that the only way one can give a representation of time is through recourse to a spatial order—a line:

Past	Present	Future

The problem with this image is not that it is entirely wrong; it is rather that it is too perfect. It is perfect in the grammatical sense of a verb in its perfect aspect, meaning that the act described by the verb has already been completed (i.e. 'I have read the book'). But to think of time in terms of something, which is finished in this way, is to misconstrue the notion of time altogether. To think of time in this way is to overlook the very process of things, events and times that are coming into being—a process that arguably is essential for the notion of time. One should understand operational time as a way of making up for this lack, which clings to the representation of chronological time with a line. According to Guillaume, operational is the time the mind takes to actualize such a (perfect or finalized) image of time. It is the potentiality out of which a constructed image of time can be generated. Operational time can, in other words, be seen as potential time. It is a form of time that can be actualized as an image of chronological time at any moment in chronological time. The meaning of chronological time is thus dual in a very specific sense. There is chronological time and then there is the possibility for each moment in chronological time that it can be made into an image of itself. This movement of chronological time onto itself, which implies its own potentiality as a surplus of itself, is what is produced by the mind in operational time. But precisely because chronological time is forced into such a movement onto itself, it is an inherently paradoxical concept:

> It is as though man, insofar as he is a thinking and speaking being produced an additional time with regard to chronological time, a time that prevented him from perfectly coinciding with the time out of which he could make images and representations (Agamben 2005b, p.67).

In the words of Shakespeare's Hamlet, the point of operational time is that time as such is 'out of joint'. Time does not fit with itself. As chronological time it is constantly exposed to its own potentiality to become identical with itself as chronological time. This potentiality of chronological time to become self-identical is what characterizes its being out of joint with itself. It is because it is never simply identical with itself, but rather always merely potentially self-identical, that it is impossible for it to fully coincide with itself.

Again we must leave the strict Aristotelian framework in order to come to terms with this idea. Instead, we enter the Bartlebyian way of thinking, if we follow Guillaume's analysis of chronological time. The point that the representation of chronological time never fully coincides with chronological time, and hence opens the space for operational time, is the point that chronological time is characterized by potentiality not-to (be fully identical with itself). Chronological time always entails the inability to fully actualize itself as chronological time; it is never quite identical to itself. This is why chronological time necessitates the introduction of operational time. Operational time is in this way nothing but the surplus (of time) introduced by the fact that chronological time cannot fully coincide with itself.

If we now return to the notion of messianism, as Agamben understands it, then it is exactly this being-out-of-joint-with-itself of time, which characterizes messianic time. The idea that time is coming to an end does not mean that the final point on the line of chronological time is approaching. Rather, it means that for each moment in chronological time, there is a possibility for the completion of a finalized time-image. That which comes to an end in messianic time is thus not the chronology as such—it is the operational time, which for each moment in chronological time can be actualized as the self-identity of chronological time. The moment where the potential self-identity of chronological time is actualized is kairos—a condensed point in time where time is brought into direct relation with itself.

In order to fully comprehend this point about the relation of chronological and operational time, it will be worthwhile to consider what it means for something to be completed. That something is completed means that its coming into being is finished. In relation to chronological time, this is the notion of the *past*. The past is the temporal modality of the things that are perfect or completed. In chronological time, the past is that which has finished its coming into being. The future, on the other hand, is the open. The future is that which is incomplete. It is that which is in the process of being actualized. In chronological time we are thus able to change the future but not the past. Agamben understands messianic time as that which inverts this relation: 'Here, the past (the complete) rediscovers actuality and becomes unfulfilled, and the present (the incomplete) acquires a kind of fulfillment' (Agamben 2005b, p.75). What is subject to change is the past rather than the present and the future.

To see how that is possible, we will have to draw one additional conclusion from Guillaume. It was said that operational time is what can occur at each moment of chronological time. This could be taken to mean that chronological time is the precondition of operational time, but in a crucial sense the very opposite is the case. This is so because chronological time is simply the representational time-image, which is produced by operational time. In other words, there can be no chronos before operational time has done its work. There is no chronos before it has been seized by kairos (Agamben 2005b, p.69). What is produced in operational time is exactly the constitutive moment, which designates the past as past and the future as future. It is only because operational time is able to create such a time-image that chronological time is at all conceivable. This is especially crucial for our understanding of the past. If chronological time is only complete in virtue of the work of operational time, then the past—which chronologically is time in its perfect aspect—is dependent upon the work of operational time as well. It is the work of the messianic moment which determines the past. The ultimate consequence of this point is that in messianic time even the past is open and in a sense changeable.

Eschatology and the notion of the eschaton is a way of thinking about time that necessarily ignores the point Agamben (and Guillaume) makes with operational time. This is so because if the notion of the eschaton is to make sense, then we need to fix the time that runs its course until the eschaton. In other words, eschatology relies on the notion of chronological time that Agamben has argued, with the aid of Guillaume, to be impossible: the perfect and broken time-image. Messianic time, on the other hand, is simply the notion of time that emerges once one takes this lesson to heart.

Eschatology is the idea of time coming to an end. It is the idea of the end of this world and the coming of a new one. The notion of messianism is entirely different. It is the notion of time that does not come to an end, but which is nevertheless (in the process of) coming to an end. It belongs to chronologically-ordered time, but it is more than that. Where eschatological time is the end (or the destruction) of chronological time, messianic time is the relation of chronological time to itself. It is a relation that, as we have seen, means that even the past is open to the free use of human beings. Messianic time is not the notion of the end of time, it is the notion of the radical open-endedness of time.

References

Agamben, G. *Homo Sacer. Sovereign Power and Bare Life*. Stanford, CA: Stanford University Press, 1998.

——. *Means Without End*. Minneapolis: University of Minnesota Press, 2000.

——. *Potentialities. Collected Essays in Philosophy.* Stanford: Stanford University Press, 1999a.

——. *Profanations*. New York: Zone Books, 2007.

——. *Remnants of Auschwitz. The Witness and the Archive*. New York: Zone Books, 1999b.

——. *State of exception*. Chicago: Chicago University Press, 2005a.

——. *The Coming Community*. Minneapolis: University of Minnesota Press, 1993.

——. *The Kingdom and the Glory*. Stanford: Stanford University Press, 2011.

——. *The Time That Remains. A Commentary on the Letter to the Romans*. Stanford: Stanford University Press, 2005b.

Aquinas, T. *Summa Theologica*. New York: Benziger B. 1947.

Arendt, H. *On Revolution*. London: Penguin Books, 1990.

Aristotle. *Metaphysics*. Michigan: Ann Arbor, 1960.

Badiou, A. 'The Adventure of French Philosophy.' *New Left Review*, 35(September - October), pp.67–77, 2005.

Benjamin, W. 'Critique of Violence'. In M. Bullock & W. Jennings, eds. *Selected Writings*, Vol. 1. Massachusetts: Belknap Harward, pp. 277–300, 1999.

——. *The Origin of German Tragic Drama*. London: Verso, 2003.

——. 'Theses on the Philosophy of History'. In *Illuminations*. New York: Schocken Books, 1968.

Butler, J. *Gender trouble: Feminism and the Subversion of Identity*. New York: Routledge, 1999.

ECHR Grand Chamber. *Case of El-Masri v. The Former Yugoslav Republic of Macedonia* (Application no. 39630/09), 2012.

Foucault, M. *Discipline and Punish. The Birth of the Prison*. New York: Vintage Books, 1995.

——. *Madness and Civilization. A History of Insanity in the Age of Reason*. New York: Vintage Books, 1964.

——. *Power: The Essential Works of Michel Foucault 1954-1984*. London: Penguin, 2002.

Gross, O. & Ní Aoláin, F. *Law in Times of Crisis. Emergency Powers in Theory and Practice*. Cambridge: Cambridge University Press, 2006.

Hobbes, T. *The Leviathan*. New York: W.W. Norton & Company, 1997.

Kelsen, H. *Wer Soll der Hüter der Verfassung sein*. Tübingen: Mohr Siebeck, 2008.

McCormick, J. *Carl Schmitt's Critique of Liberalism*. Cambridge: Cambridge University Press, 1997.

Melville, H. *Bartleby the Scrivener*. Pymble: HarperCollins, 2009.

Murray, A. & Zartaloudis, T. 'The Power of Thought.' *Law and Critique*, 20(3), pp.207–210, 2009.

Negri, A. *Insurgencies: Constituent Power and the Modern State*, Minneapolis: University of Minnesota Press, 1999.

Nussbaum, M. 'The Supreme Court, 2006 Term, Foreword: Constitutions and Capabilities: "Perception" against Lofty Formalism.' *Harward Law Review*, 121(4), pp.4–97, 2007.

Nussbaum, M. & Sen, A. *The Quality of Life*. Oxford: Clarendon, 1993.

Scheuerman, W. 'Survey Article: Emergency Powers and the Rule of Law After 9/11'. *The Journal of Political Philosophy*, 14(1), pp.61–84, 2006.

Schmitt, C. *Dictatorship*. Cambridge: Polity, 2013.

——. *Political Theology*. Chicago: University of Chicago Press, 1985.

——. *The Leviathan in the State Theory of Thomas Hobbes*. Chicago: University of Chicago Press, 2008.

——. *The Nomos of the Earth. In the International Law of the Jus Publicum Europaeum*. New York: Telos Press, 2003.

Ugilt, R. *The Metaphysics of Terror*. New York: Bloomsbury, 2012.

Vermeule, A. 'Libertarian Panics'. *Rutgers L.J.*, 36, pp.871–888, 2005.

About the Author

Rasmus Ugilt is Assistant Professor in Philosophy at the Department of Culture and Society, Aarhus University, Denmark. filru@cas. au.dk

His main research interests are classic German philosophy (Kant, Hegel, and Schelling), contemporary continental philosophy (Agamben, Badiou, Butler, Deleuze, Dolar, Žižek, Zupančič) and political and legal philosophy focusing especially on the political and legal situation that has emerged as a result of the anti-terrorism politicies that dominated international politics in the first decade of the new millennium. He is the author of *The Metaphysics of Terror* (New York: Bloomsbury, 2012).

Humanities-Ebooks.co.uk

Some Academic titles

Sibylle Baumbach, *Shakespeare and the Art of Physiognomy*

John Beer, *Blake's Humanism*

John Beer, *The Achievement of E M Forster*

John Beer, *Coleridge the Visionary*

Jared Curtis, ed., *The Fenwick Notes of William Wordsworth**

Jared Curtis, ed., *The Cornell Wordsworth: A Supplement**

Steven Duncan, *Analytic Philosophy of Religion: its History since 1955**

John K Hale, *Milton as Multilingual: Selected Essays 1982–2004*

Simon Hull, ed., *The British Periodical Text, 1797–1835*

Rob Johnson, Mark Levene and Penny Roberts, eds., *History at the End of the World **

John Lennard, *Modern Dragons and other Essays on Genre Fiction**

C W R D Moseley, *Shakespeare's History Plays*

Paul McDonald, *Laughing at the Darkness: Postmodernism and American Humour **

Colin Nicholson, *Fivefathers: Interviews with late Twentieth-Century Scottish Poets*

W J B Owen, *Understanding 'The Prelude'*

Pamela Perkins, ed., *Francis Jeffrey's Highland and Continental Tours**

Keith Sagar, *D. H. Lawrence: Poet**

Reinaldo Francisco Silva, *Portuguese American Literature**

William Wordsworth, *Concerning the Convention of Cintra**

W J B Owen and J W Smyser, eds., *Wordsworth's Political Writings**

The Poems of William Wordsworth: Collected Reading Texts from the Cornell Wordsworth, 3 vols.*

* These titles are also available in print using links from
http://www.humanities-ebooks.co.uk

Humanities Insights

These are some of the Insights available at:
http://www.humanities-ebooks.co.uk/

General Titles

An Introduction to Critical Theory
Modern Feminist Theory
An Introduction to Rhetorical Terms

Genre FictionSightlines

Octavia E Butler: *Xenogenesis / Lilith's Brood*
Reginal Hill: *On Beulah's Height*
Ian McDonald: *Chaga / Evolution's Store*
Walter Mosley: *Devil in a Blue Dress*
Tamora Pierce: *The Immortals*
Tamora Pierce: *Protector of the Small*

History Insights

Oliver Cromwell
The British Empire: Pomp, Power and Postcolonialism
The Holocaust: Events, Motives, Legacy
Lenin's Revolution
Methodism and Society
The Risorgimento

Literature Insights

Austen: *Emma*
Conrad: *The Secret Agent*
T S Eliot: 'The Love Song of J Alfred Prufrock' and *The Waste Land*
English Renaissance Drama: Theatre and Theatres in Shakespeare's Time
Faulkner: *Go Down, Moses* and *Big Woods'*
Faulkner: *The Sound and the Fury*
Gaskell, *Mary Barton*
Hardy: *Tess of the Durbervilles*
Heller: *Catch-22*
Ibsen: *The Doll's House*
Hopkins: Selected Poems
Hughes: *New Selected Poems*
Larkin: *Selected Poems*
Lawrence: Selected Short Stories
Lawrence: *Sons and Lovers*
Lawrence: *Women in Love*

Morrison: *Beloved*
Scott: *The Raj Quartet*
Shakespeare: *Hamlet*
Shakespeare: *Henry IV*
Shakespeare: *King Lear*
Shakespeare: *Richard II*
Shakespeare: *Richard III*
Shakespeare: *The Merchant of Venice*
Shakespeare: *The Tempest*
Shakespeare: *Troilus and Cressida*
Shelley: *Frankenstein*
Toomer: *Cane*
Wordsworth: *Lyrical Ballads*
Fields of Agony: English Poetry and the First World War

Philosophy Insights

Agamben
American Pragmatism
Barthes
Thinking Ethically about Business
Critical Thinking
Existentialism
Formal Logic
Metaethics
Contemporary Philosophy of Religion
Philosophy of Sport
Plato
Wittgenstein
Žižek

Some Titles in Preparation

Rousseau's legacy
Dreiser: *Sister Carrie*
Fitzgerald: *The Great Gatsby*
Heaney: Selected Poems
James: *The Ambassadors*
Melville: *Moby-Dick*
Melville: Three Novellas
Shakespeare: *Romeo and Juliet*

Printed in Great Britain
by Amazon